OTHER BOOKS BY JOHN COLEMAN

Questions from Your Cosmic Dance

The UNEXPECTED
TEACHINGS
of JESUS

The UNEXPECTED TEACHINGS *of* JESUS

Encountering the Gospels All Over Again

JOHN COLEMAN

JOSSEY-BASS
A Wiley Company
www.josseybass.com

Published by

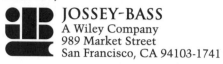

JOSSEY-BASS
A Wiley Company
989 Market Street
San Francisco, CA 94103-1741

www.josseybass.com

Copyright © 2002 by John Wiley & Sons, Inc.
Jossey-Bass is a registered trademark of John Wiley & Sons, Inc.

Jossey-Bass books and products are available through most bookstores. To contact Jossey-Bass directly, call (888) 378–2537, fax to (800) 605–2665, or visit our Web site at www.josseybass.com.

Substantial discounts on bulk quantities of Jossey-Bass books are available to corporations, professional associations, and other organizations. For details and discount information, contact the special sales department at Jossey-Bass.

We at Jossey-Bass strive to use the most environmentally sensitive paper stocks available to us. Our publications are printed on acid-free recycled stock whenever possible, and our paper always meets or exceeds minimum GPO and EPA requirements.

The Scripture quotations contained herein (unless otherwise noted) are from the New Revised Standard Version Bible, copyright, 1989, by the Division of Christian Education of the National Council of the Churches of Christ in the U.S.A. Used by permission. All rights reserved.

Credits appear on page 240.

Library of Congress Cataloging-in-Publication Data

Coleman, John, date.
The unexpected teachings of Jesus: encountering the Gospels all over again/
John Coleman.
  p. cm.
Includes bibliographical references and index.
  ISBN 0–7879–5983–9 (alk. paper)
  1. Jesus Christ—Teachings. 2. Bible. N.T. Gospels—Criticism, interpretation, etc.
  I. Title.
BS2415 .C57 2002
226'.06—dc21   2001004898

FIRST EDITION
HB Printing   10 9 8 7 6 5 4 3 2 1

CONTENTS

ACKNOWLEDGMENTS

For the better part of my life, I've been a Christian. Like many folks, I've been in loads of Sunday school classes, heard hundreds of sermons, and engaged in countless conversations. When I add to this my seminary studies and experiences in ministry, I'm aware that dozens of relationships and hundreds of hours of sharing and reflection form the foundation of my writing and thinking.

I owe a great debt to many people, more than I have space to mention here. The unexpected teachings of Jesus are not simply my own discovery. Significant hunks as well as bits and pieces belong to wise teachers, colleagues, and friends. I do want to mention several folks who deserve a special word of thanks for introducing me to some of Jesus' unexpected teachings:

- Thanks to Mark Allan Powell for the insights upon which "The Bruised Harvest" and "The Wicked, the Gnarled, and the Wounded" are based.

- ⚹ Thanks to Donald G. Luck for teaching me about the *malkuth shamayim* and helping me to see that God is "doing heaven" all around us.
- ⚹ Thanks to Cheryl Corneluissen for the observation that led to "The Lord's Prayer."
- ⚹ Thanks to Trinity Lutheran Seminary in Columbus, Ohio, the community that in many ways gave life to this book.

Whatever wisdom you might find in the meditations listed above is due to these folks. If you find any fault or foolishness, charge it to my account, not theirs.

Finally, I want to thank several folks who have helped bring this book to life in a way particularly meaningful to me. Sheryl Fullerton, senior editor at Jossey-Bass, has shared with me her insight, intuition, good sense, and kindness, all of which have been blessings to me and to this book. Eric Anderson was one of the first readers of the manuscript, and his support and suggestions came to me at a crucial point in the writing journey. My running partner, Chad Johnson, was a sounding board for me as we rumbled down the road. Coffee Partners and friends Jim Fravel, Gary Harris, Bob Hegdal, Vince Lyons, and Jeff Otterman somehow seemed to be present at just the right moment with a helpful word. And my wife, Kathy, has read and proofread more drafts than is fair for any husband to ask. To her and to our kids, Elena and Micah, I give not only love but also this book. Were home not a place of peace, stability, and nourishment, I wouldn't have had the heart to write. Thanks.

INTRODUCTION

My eleven-year-old daughter, Elena, and seven-year-old son, Micah, and I are pounding down lunch at the Taipei. We all have chicken: sweet and sour, honey and garlic, and General Tso's. It's Wednesday, my day off over the summer as I work on this book, so the kids and I are spending a few bucks and having some fun. My wife, Kathy, is at work, building office furniture.

Outside, the July heat takes our breath away and makes us feel claustrophobic and disoriented, so we're glad to be inside the cool restaurant, grazing away, drinking Chinese tea, just hanging out together and joking around. About midway through the meal, I notice what's always the case with Elena and Micah eating Chinese food: they're scarfing down the chicken and leaving the vegetables and rice. I put some rice on each of their plates and lovingly insist. Micah picks up a piece of General Tso's with his fingers, licks off some stray rice, then munches it down. He's avoiding the inevitable.

"Micah," I say, "you've got to eat some rice."

"Do they have to eat all this rice in China, too?" he says back.

Aha, my overly serious mind says to itself, *a teaching moment.* Now, I don't pretend to be an expert on the social or cultural realities of China, but it occurs to me how telling Micah's question is. I once heard on a cooking program (yes, I know, the cornerstone of scholarly reliability) that folks in China tend to load up on the rice and basically use a few pieces of meat and sauce as a condiment. This jibes with my own observation. I've frequented a number of Chinese restaurants and seen those who work there eat lunch—always a big bowl of rice with a couple of chunks of meat on top.

"Micah," I say, "you know, in China, most people eat a whole bunch of rice and a little bit of chicken."

He looks at me as if I have three heads.

"Yeah," I go on, "chicken's more expensive than the rice, and lots of people can afford just a small piece of meat to go with their rice. So you're asking if they have to eat a whole bunch of rice. What they might say is, 'I hope there's enough rice for me.'"

I say all this quietly, patiently. I'm not being a heavy. The topic changes to the number of cups of Chinese tea loaded with sugar an eleven- and seven-year-old can drink before getting a case of the shakes.

It must be tough having a dad who thinks too much.

Who I am affects how I see things. Micah has more than enough to eat, so much, in fact, that he feels compelled to rank the courses of each meal from best to worst. He doesn't know what it means to wonder if he'll be hungry when his head hits the pillow tonight. Many nights, for that matter, he grabs a quick cuddle before heading into his own bed, so he literally drifts off to sleep still feeling the warmth of his father's arms around him and kisses on top of his head. This, too, impacts the way he sees the world.

It's not too far a leap to suppose that, for all of us, the amount of food in our refrigerators, the balance in our checking accounts, and the extent to which we feel loved and embraced affect not only the gratefulness with which we approach the dinner table but also our modus operandi for engaging the world. What's especially struck me over the past few years is how such matters as wealth, health, habits, and self-image impact the way we read the Bible. When I sit down to do my morning devotions and read Scripture, my status as a middle-class, white, thirty-something Lutheran pastor and former college English professor living in the United States leads me to read the Old and New Testaments in a way different from that of a thirty-something poor Nicaraguan woman. Stories she would cherish I would read right past and vice versa. For example, such a woman might center her life and faith upon the following words from the Magnificat:

He has brought down the powerful from their
thrones,
> and lifted up the lowly;
he has filled the hungry with good things,
> and sent the rich away empty. (LUKE 1:52–53)

I, on the other hand, might be tempted to under-value such verses because, at least compared to this Nicaraguan woman, I'm quite rich financially.

So who I am makes me fall in love with particular moments of Scripture and underestimate or ignore altogether other moments. In this book, I'm trying to tease into awareness those details in Scripture, specifically in the Gospels, that I—and many of us—tend to ignore because of where we're from, when we live, what we have, and how we've been taught. When we're able to get outside ourselves just a bit, to read accounts of Jesus' life and ministry without assuming that we're the center of the universe, again and again Jesus teaches us something unexpected. And, ironically, these unexpected teachings, far from being simply interesting or amusing, are precisely what we need to inspire and guide us in prayer, reflection, and action.

This collection of meditations on Jesus' unexpected teachings is broken up into several parts that themselves deserve a few words of introduction. "The Blindside Teachings" focus on incidents in the Gospels that invite us to think in a way that's just the opposite of what we're used to. Here, Jesus' teachings hit us—gently most of the time—from a direction we hadn't been looking. "The (Re)Visionary Teachings" nudge us to revise our takes on some issues about which we may be a bit too content and settled and, in so doing, to adjust our vision of Jesus and the life to which he calls us. "The Shalom Teachings" are especially of interest as people try to live together in a healthy, honest, peaceful fashion. When we manage to do so, we may taste *shalom:* wholeness, love, and a measure of prosperity in our communion with God and one another. "The Perilous Teachings" have a risky feel to them because they address concepts that may be difficult or painful to accept and apply. Every honest book about Christianity—and this is one—needs to sit a while at the foot of the cross. Finally, "The Restorative Teachings" offer pointers on how to live and think as well-adjusted, faithful Christians. Jesus' lessons in this chapter are therapeutic surprises. After each meditation, I've included a section entitled "Invitation to Reflection," should you or a group of your friends want to have some starting points for conversation.

I don't pretend to have exhausted all the possibilities of Jesus' unexpected teachings or even to have hit upon the most urgent ones in each text. Rather, these meditations offer some lessons from the Gospels that I often miss and need to hear. I hope you find in the pages ahead what you need to hear as well.

For Kathy, Elena, and Micah
And in memory of my mother, Dolores Coleman

The UNEXPECTED
TEACHINGS
of JESUS

The BLINDSIDE

TEACHINGS

"For those who want to save

their life will lose it,

and those who lose their life for my sake,

and for the sake of the gospel,

will save it." (MARK 8:35)

LEAVING THE CATCH BEHIND

Luke 5:1–11

¹Once while Jesus was standing beside the lake of Gennesaret and the crowd was pressing in on him to hear the word of God, ²he saw two boats there at the shore of the lake; the fishermen had gone out of them and were washing their nets. ³He got into one of the boats, the one belonging to Simon, and asked him to put out a little way from the shore. Then he sat down and taught the crowds from the boat. ⁴When he had finished speaking, he said to Simon, "Put out into the deep water and let down your nets for a catch." ⁵Simon answered, "Master, we have worked all night long but have caught nothing. Yet if you say so, I will let down the nets." ⁶When they had done this, they caught so many fish that their nets were beginning to break. ⁷So they signaled their partners in the other boat to come and help them. And they came and filled both boats, so that they began to sink. ⁸But when Simon Peter saw it, he fell down at Jesus' knees, saying, "Go away from me, Lord, for I am a sinful man!" 9For he and all who were with him were amazed at the catch of fish that they had taken; 10and so also were James and John, sons of Zebedee, who were partners with Simon. Then Jesus said to Simon, "Do not be afraid; from now on you will be catching people." 11When they had brought their boats to shore, they left everything and followed him.

❊ ❊ ❊

THE UNEXPECTED TEACHING:

Simon Peter, James, and John walked away from their miracle.

As I write this meditation in Columbus, Ohio, eleven coworkers at a factory less than an hour away try to figure out what to do with their share of over two hundred million dollars they won in the lottery. If anyone doubts that Western culture loves a good miracle, the phenomenon of swelling lottery jackpots and folks willing to wait in line for hours in hopes of being the lucky ones ought to put any skepticism to rest. Of course, it's not just miracles we love but also easy answers to life's struggles. When we can't have a straightforward blast of good fortune (like a ten-million-dollar, two- by four-foot check, a team of cameras, and two guys smiling broadly showing up at our doorstep to catch us in our bathrobes as television viewers watch us quiver with delight), we want, and have come to expect, at least a quick fix: cosmetic surgeons can slurp out from under our skin the fat from years of late-night binges, and we can buy thousands of dollars' worth of possessions with only a hunk of plastic and a promise.

For these reasons, Luke's story of the miraculous catch of fish is perfect for our age and for well-intentioned Christians. If we but listen to Jesus, the reasoning goes, we ought to be hooking our own jackpot one of these days. Maybe we hope for our own kettle of money, a smashing physique in middle age, a house our friends will marvel at, a killer car to climb out of as we toss the keys to the valet. It's easy to understand why we dream such dreams. Life is tough; it would be nice to think that the difficult realities of being human could somehow be eliminated by something we can touch—a check, a lean body, a Mercedes-Benz.

As I suspect we all know in the quiet crannies of our hearts, happiness isn't something we can grab with our hands. But there's good news. Although our existence can't be rendered blissful by the accumulation of stuff, we ourselves can be transformed. That's a neglected teaching of Luke's story of the miraculous catch. The last line reads, "When they had brought their boats to shore, they left everything and followed him." What Simon Peter, James, and John did was like forgetting to pick up their lottery check. They left their great big, impossible, extravagant gift flopping around on the beach and walked off after Jesus because they sensed in him a quality that transcends the material.

And that's the point. Luke's version of the catch story would have us love and follow the one from whom extravagance flows more than the raw matter of extravagance. We love Jesus, the miraculous one, the human face of God's radical self-giving, and we gratefully accept whatever gift we are given. But make no mistake, at the first word from Jesus, we leave the gift itself in the dust.

Does this mean that lottery winners ought to tear up their checks? I sure wouldn't. I love Jesus, but I'm not stupid. What we all should do—winners and losers alike—is keep our eyes on Jesus, not on the dollar signs. When we focus on Jesus and try to figure out what he calls us to do and who he calls us to be, we open ourselves to the possibility of living daily within the jackpot.

The canopy of trees outside the front door, with sun streaming through the branches: all these years it's been there, a gift from God, and we've never looked up because we're too busy hoping for something wonderful to transport us from our present situation. The silence of the evening: forever, it has been trying to give itself to us, but instead we've been listening to some polished guy on television telling us how our lives depend on what he's selling. Loved ones looking into our eyes: they've drifted in and out of our days. God has been wanting to use them to look upon us and to receive our loving gaze in return, but we've resisted intimacy.

When we journey with the one who radiates grace, glorious surprises (and, yes, hard challenges) are around each bend. But the real miracle, the heart of mystery, the never-ending blood rush of all wonders, is Jesus the Christ. We give ourselves to him, not to the check or the fish.

Invitation to Reflection ✂

✘ Liposuction, lotteries, and longings: most of us hang on to some "if only" dreams—*If only I had more money, If only I could get rid of this knackwurst around my waist, If only I could get this person I love to open up to me, to let me in.* The trick is distinguishing healthy, productive dreams from fantasies of escape, which tend to masquerade as God. Can you name your fantasies of escape?

✘ Imagine how your life would be if those escapist fantasies never came true. Is it possible to slowly let go of them—if you know that God stands ready to fill in the empty space they leave behind?

✘ How might life actually be better without fantasies of escape?

THE EYES OF PRAYER

Luke 5:12–16

¹²Once, when he was in one of the cities, there was a man covered with leprosy. When he saw Jesus, he bowed with his face to the ground and begged him, "Lord, if you choose, you can make me clean." ¹³Then Jesus stretched out his hand, touched him, and said, "I do choose. Be made clean." Immediately the leprosy left him. ¹⁴And he ordered him to tell no one. "Go," he said, "and show yourself to the priest, and, as Moses commanded, make an offering for your cleansing, for a testimony to them." ¹⁵But now more than ever the word about Jesus spread abroad; many crowds would gather to hear him and to be cured of their diseases. ¹⁶But he would withdraw to deserted places and pray.

❧ ❧ ❧

THE UNEXPECTED TEACHING:
Jesus set aside regular time for prayer—
especially when he got busy.

Asides and afterthoughts are packed with information. In ten years of talking with struggling college students, I learned as much about the roots of their difficulties by paying attention to their innocent comments as I did by focusing on the gist of what they were saying. It was what they said when they thought they were finished talking that told their real stories. As their voices trailed off, they mumbled something about hating reading or being stressed out by a breakup or getting sick of all the noise in the dormitory—then I knew I'd hit pay dirt. At that point, the student and I would start picking at the packaging that was concealing the root problem, which was as often personal as academic.

Like the afterthoughts of my students, the last few innocent words of this episode from Luke offer a message that's just as powerful as the central event, perhaps more so, given our culture's addiction to work and activity. In the previous chapters of Luke's Gospel, Jesus was busy—getting baptized, tempted, and rejected at Nazareth, and preaching and healing like, if you'll pardon the expression, a man possessed. Word got around about Jesus. Folks wanted to hear what he had to say, and everybody with any condition from paralysis to indigestion was trying to lay a hand on his tunic. Jesus' moment had come. Business was booming. "Now more than ever," the passage goes, "word about Jesus spread abroad." So what did Jesus do? Did he roll up his sleeves and work twenty hours per day as he probably could have? No. Just when we would expect Jesus to put in longer hours, he went off alone to pray. And the phrasing "he would withdraw to deserted places and pray" suggests a habit, not a one-time action.

Why make a big deal about Jesus' finding a place alone to pray when things were getting busy? Because our culture's failure to do so is tearing apart individuals and families. We believe that there's no time to let up in our schedules, so we neglect our own need for prayerful rest and fail to see the impact our weariness has on our relationships. Some people blame what they see as a moral decline in the United States for marriages breaking up, but I wonder how many married couples (and their kids) suffer because they have little energy to be fully present, attentive, and loving to one another. And where does such energy come from? Jesus' actions teach us that we don't have our own bottomless reservoir of love and healing to draw from. We have to go off by ourselves and pray if we want to know the gifts of the Spirit.

If we take seriously the call to prayer implicit in this story of Jesus' cleansing the leper, then we had better get ready for a domino effect, for the call to prayer is also a call to open ourselves to God's word and to reflect on its guidance for our behavior. I know of nobody who has committed to increasing (or establishing) time for daily prayer who has not also seen her or his priorities change. Those who "withdraw to deserted places and pray" experience a deepening of their relationships with others, an awakening to sacred moments, and a strengthening of their personal character.

In other words, the eyes of the prayerful are gradually opened to the abundant wealth in what can't be bought. All the clichés like "Money can't buy me love" and "Stop and smell the roses" are absolutely true, and prayerful folks know this in their souls and bellies, not just in their heads. That's the domino effect: in reading Scripture and reflecting upon the life of Christ, the prayerful person slowly understands the real cost of always being on the move, of always working hard and then making play a labor as well, of rushing from one obligation to another, of crowding a home with possession upon possession: the cost is life.

And so the prayerful person tries to slow down. It may take years. It may be barely perceptible at first. A mother has been praying daily for a month. She holds her six-year-old son when he comes in from playing to get a drink on a sticky August afternoon. She feels his sweaty hair against her cheek. She really holds him. She can still feel his small body in her arms after he bolts back outside. She walks to the window, watches the way he swings his arms when he runs. She says to God: "Thank you for this moment, for trusting me to take care of this boy, for letting me have this gift, even for just today."

Or a husband has been praying daily for a little over a year. Late one evening, when he's just ready to go to bed, his wife says, "Want to have some coffee?" He says,

"Sure." As they sit together, he turns toward her and listens as she talks about her day. He turns off the television. He's not pretending to listen; he's really listening. She doesn't know why he seems so attentive. Deep in her chest, from where a cry might come, she feels joy for an instant as she looks at him. He has given her a gift.

Jesus knows gifts. He teaches us that no matter how busy we are, we have to pray and open our hearts and minds to the reality of God's presence. Jesus teaches us that without prayer there is no cleansing, no healing, no gathering, no hearing, no meaningful choosing.

When our schedules are crowded with activity from morning until night, God calls us, now more than ever, to discover a new first order of business: find a quiet place and pray.

Invitation to Reflection

- I invite you to stop for a moment. Do you feel trapped within your life, like your days are all prepoured into spandex pants?

- Take a look at your daily responsibilities and activities. How much time do you spend tending to your relationship with God—or letting God tend to you? (The purpose of this is not to bring about a guilt trip but to do a reality check.)

- Many people find that the only way they pray with any regularity is if they make it part of their routine. Could you find twenty minutes in your daily rhythm for prayer? When exactly might that time be? First thing in the morning? Over lunch in the privacy of an office?

For Further Reading

As you read this, you might be making a decision to set aside prayer time. If so, you might be feeling unsure of how to begin. Fortunately, folks write entire books on this very topic. Here are a few treatments I've found helpful: *The Presence of Absence* by Doris Grumbach; *Open Mind, Open Heart* by Father Thomas Keating; *The New Seeds of Contemplation* by Thomas Merton; and *Peace Is Every Step* by Thich Nhat Hanh (this last book offers prayerful practices that aren't Christian but are in harmony with Jesus' teachings).

THE BRUISED
HARVEST

Matthew 9:35–10:8

9 *35 Then Jesus went about all the cities and villages, teaching in their synagogues, and proclaiming the good news of the kingdom, and curing every disease and every sickness. 36 When he saw the crowds, he had compassion for them, because they were harassed and helpless, like sheep without a shepherd. 37 Then he said to his disciples, "The harvest is plentiful, but the laborers are few; 38 therefore ask the Lord of the harvest to send out laborers into his harvest."*

10 *1 Then Jesus summoned his twelve disciples and gave them authority over unclean spirits, to cast them out, and to cure every disease and every sickness. 2 These are the names of the twelve apostles: first, Simon, also known as Peter, and his brother Andrew; James son of Zebedee, and his brother John; 3 Philip and Bartholomew; Thomas and Matthew the tax col-*

*lector; James son of Alphaeus, and Thaddaeus; 4Simon the
Cananaean, and Judas Iscariot, the one who betrayed him.*

*5These twelve Jesus sent out with the following instruc-
tions: "Go nowhere among the Gentiles, and enter no town of
the Samaritans, 6but go rather to the lost sheep of the house of
Israel. 7As you go, proclaim the good news, 'The kingdom of
heaven has come near.' 8Cure the sick, raise the dead, cleanse
the leper, cast out demons. You received without payment; give
without payment."*

✶ ✶ ✶

The Unexpected Teaching:
Jesus' harvest was people who were suffering.

Voltaire writes, "If God created us in his own
image, we have more than reciprocated." Applied to
Scripture, this point suggests that we read selectively,
focusing on images that most closely resemble the picture of God that we have rendered in our own image.
This impulse to read the Bible in the fashion that suits us
best is almost inescapable. Unless we are hyper-aware of
who we are and what drives our engines, we get swept
away in using God's word as an instrument to suit our
own purposes.

I think this particular phenomenon often takes place
when church folks read this scriptural passage. We love
to lift up the harvest as a metaphor for bringing people
into our churches. We encourage laborers to go into the
field and gather in the harvest, telling ourselves that we

want to bring people to Jesus but too often wanting to fill our pews. In fact, nowhere in the vicinity of this story did Jesus talk about getting members for churches.

What Jesus did do in the two chapters leading up to the harvest quotation was heal people. Starting in Chapter Eight, Jesus healed a leper, a centurion's servant, Peter's mother-in-law and a whole crowd at Peter's house, the Gadarene demoniacs, a paralytic, a hemorrhaging woman, two blind men, and a mute. In between there, he raised a girl from the dead.

Right before he talked about the harvest, Jesus looked out on a crowd that the writer of Matthew describes as "harassed and helpless." Then he summoned the Twelve and gave them a job, presumably in response to the frenzy of healing he'd just done and the crowd of lost people he'd just seen. The job: "proclaim the good news, 'The kingdom of heaven has come near.' Cure the sick, raise the dead, cleanse the leper, cast out demons." And, Jesus said, do it all for free.

So the question is, What is the harvest? Obviously, it's a metaphor, but what exactly does it stand for? If the harvest is people, then who are these people? The quick easy answer is, All of us. Well, yeah, kind of. But specifically, the context suggests that Jesus was thinking of people who were sick in mind or body or harassed or helpless in their circumstances. It's not difficult to understand why Jesus would have singled such people out as deserving attention. Who in Jesus' day would have suffered more than those who were physically and mentally ill? Imagine the ailments we can diagnose today that must have terrorized Jesus' contemporaries, the simple infections a round of antibiotics would tackle today that would have killed folks slowly and painfully. Or imagine a common psychological condition like manic depression that might have sent a person into exile from family and friends.

Yet Jesus called such people a harvest, that which is to be gathered in and prized as the abundant livelihood and treasure of the farmer. The implication is that those who suffered were precious to Jesus. They were to be embraced and valued. They were, in fact, the focus of the disciples' mission.

The Twelve certainly wouldn't have struggled to figure out where to look for their charges. Their instructions were clear, and the work was all around them. Discerning how this particular mission translates to our present situation is perhaps a little less clear. For one thing, most churches don't think it is their mission to go out and heal people of their diseases. Medical science has demystified much for us. Then again, maybe we're wrong. Maybe we ought to be laying hands on the sick and expecting their illnesses to disappear. I'm not being flippant here; I'm just not sure.

In any case, we have to ask ourselves, Who would Jesus be identifying as the harvest today? Who around us are the harassed and helpless? Who are the sick, dead, or possessed? Who is today's leper? Who are the bruised and battered? If the church is to heed God's call and send out laborers into the harvest, it needs to consider these questions. The church—as international, national, and regional bodies, as well as each local congregation—is called to discern them as well. Finally, individual Christians might well wonder who among this harvest lives next door to or works with them.

The mission, then, is not to fill the pews but to seek out the person who is helpless, the leper whom our society keeps in caves at the edge of town, the neighbor who is dead in spirit, the coworker who is possessed. We are to tell these folks the good news, "The kingdom of heaven has come near." So we try to figure out who the harvest is and speak to these folks in ways that help them to know God's presence and unconditional love for them and act in ways that help to end their suffering.

Invitation to Reflection ❧

🖋 One way of trying to figure out whom Jesus would think of as harassed and helpless today is to look around us (suffering people are everywhere). Another approach is to look within ourselves and ask hard questions: Who makes you very uncomfortable? Are there any groups of people who tend to make you angry? Are there people with whom you prefer not to associate? Chances are, such people are a part of God's harvest. Be bold to name, at least to yourself, the members of God's harvest whom you participate in rejecting, even if only through feelings you keep to yourself.

🖋 If you knew that it was part of your mission in life to reach out lovingly to those you've named, how might that change your feelings toward them?

🖋 Is there one member of God's harvest you might touch today or someday soon?

DANCING THROUGH SABBATH GRAINFIELDS

Mark 2:23–28

²³ *One sabbath he was going through the grainfields; and as they made their way his disciples began to pluck heads of grain.* ²⁴ *The Pharisees said to him, "Look, why are they doing what is not lawful on the sabbath?"* ²⁵ *And he said to them, "Have you never read what David did when he and his companions were hungry and in need of food?* ²⁶ *He entered the house of God, when Abiathar was high priest, and ate the bread of the Presence, which it is not lawful for any but the priests to eat, and he gave some to his companions."* ²⁷ *Then he said to them, "The sabbath was made for humankind, and not humankind for the sabbath;* ²⁸ *so the Son of Man is lord even of the sabbath."*

❊ ❊ ❊

The Unexpected Teaching:
*The Sabbath was supposed to be a gift,
not a burden.*

We human beings have a mystifying ability to turn blessings into curses. The huge orange inflatable ball my wife and I bought for our kids is a great example. This thing is so big that it can't fit through a doorway without major squeezing and turning. Once it gets outside, all the kids in the neighborhood want to take a turn bouncing on top of the ball as long as they can before they go sailing onto the grass. The fun never lasts, though. They always end up flailing about in an angry dance, howling about so-and-so hogging the ball or popping veins in their skinny necks over missing a turn. So back inside the ball comes, where it sits like a huge, genetically engineered orange in the living room until I muscle it back into the basement.

Lots of other material examples abound. An old friend of mine always used to have a shiny Corvette (a different one every couple of years) in his garage but finally gave up that expensive hobby when a child put a huge scratch on the driver's-side door. It occurred to him that the 'Vettes only sat there most of the time, and they caused him more worry than pleasure. I suspect new carpeting has the same effect on people, as does a new sofa or set of dishware. When we stop to think about it, many things in our lives that ought to make us happy end up furrowing our brows and strangling our stomachs.

This is what has happened to the gift of the Sabbath. We've fretted a blessing right into a curse. Pharisees of all times and places have spent so much psychological energy following Sabbath law down to the last jot and tittle that the joy of the day got sucked right out. In fact, by following all the little laws so closely, they unwittingly demeaned the big law: the Sabbath is a day set apart for worship and rest, a day given to us so that we can center ourselves in God's word and sacrament and find refreshment for living out our call to discipleship.

The fact that "Remember the sabbath day, and keep it holy" is the third commandment makes it difficult for Western culture to view the Sabbath as a gift. Any time we are given a law or commandment, our individualistic sensibilities get inflamed, our lips purse, and we decide then and there that our freedom is being threatened. Then we go on a technicality hunt and weasel our way out of obedience.

It is true, we are commanded to "Remember the sabbath day, and keep it holy," but the wording here is crucial. We are to remember and keep the Sabbath, not worship it. When the anxiety we experience over observing it overshadows the joy of worship and prevents rest for our minds and bodies, then we are not keeping the Sabbath holy, no matter how careful we might be while walking through grainfields. We have turned the gift into a burden. As Jesus teaches in the passage above, "The sabbath was created for humankind, and not humankind for the sabbath."

But here is where the discussion gets tricky. If the Sabbath is a gift, it sure doesn't have many takers. Why is it that few of us are willing to set aside one day when we spend time with loved ones, rest our bodies, and give ourselves a break from accomplishing things? The reason is that most of us are more comfortable working, keeping busy, than sitting still. We are addicted to motion, activity. When we pause for a moment, as we might on the Sabbath, we feel like a car going sixty-five miles per hour and suddenly shifted into first gear. We lurch and wheeze. So we justify not accepting the blessing by rationalizing our familiar ways: "My mind will be much more restful," we say, "once I get this work project finished, or this carpet vacuumed, or this workout done." The fact is that when we slow down, we begin to discover that we're lost, and our minds and digestive tracts race. When we can't stand the churning any longer, we indulge our addiction rather than drag our personal beasts out of the corner and look them over.

As creatures of our culture, then, we transform the blessing of the Sabbath into a curse. It's plain scary to remember the Sabbath and keep it holy because when we do so, we understand that we are not God and neither are all the scrawny, lying little gods we buy, sell, and chase over the face of the earth. Fortunately, the good thing about taking the frightening step of observing the Sabbath is that once we sit still long enough, the false gods stop swarming around our troubled heads—or at least slow down a bit—and we start to glimpse the real God who's been waiting our whole lives to show us the central reality of being: God's love of and faithfulness to all creation.

This is the weird miracle that God works for us. When we accept *a* gift we've been resisting, the Sabbath, we receive *the* gift, the knowledge of God's love and faithfulness in the person of Jesus the Christ. On the other hand, when we surround ourselves with blessings of our own devising, all we do is binge in cosmic candy. We fly for a moment but quickly crash. In Sabbath rest, God dances with us, feeding us the grain we really need, and our spirits soar.

Invitation to Reflection

- Do you feel guilty when you take time for yourself to recharge? If so, why do you suppose you feel this way? Buddhist peace activist Thich Nhat Hanh has a helpful saying: "Don't just do something. Sit there."

- Take your calendar and block off one hour at some point during the week just to relax, take a walk alone or with a person you love, or sit on a beach or in the woods.

- Name one thing that would be life-giving to you. Is there a particular reason that you're unable to seek that thing out and enjoy it?

Barefoot and Vulnerable

John 13:1–20

¹ Now before the festival of the Passover, Jesus knew that his hour had come to depart from this world and go to the Father. Having loved his own who were in the world, he loved them to the end. ² The devil had already put it into the heart of Judas son of Simon Iscariot to betray him. And during supper ³ Jesus, knowing that the Father had given all things into his hands, and that he had come from God and was going to God, ⁴ got up from the table, took off his outer robe, and tied a towel around himself. ⁵ Then he poured water into a basin and began to wash the disciples' feet and to wipe them with the towel that was tied around him. ⁶ He came to Simon Peter, who said to him, "Lord, are you going to wash my feet?" ⁷ Jesus answered, "You do not know now what I am doing, but later you will understand." ⁸Peter said to him, "You will never wash my feet." Jesus answered, "Unless I wash you, you have no share with me." ⁹Simon Peter said to him, "Lord, not my feet only but also my hands and my head!" ¹⁰Jesus said to him, "One who has bathed does not need to wash, except for the feet, but is entirely clean. And you are clean, though not all of you." ¹¹For he knew who was to betray him; for this reason he said, "Not all of you are clean."

¹²After he had washed their feet, had put on his robe, and had returned to the table, he said to them, "Do you know what I have done to you? ¹³You call me Teacher and Lord—and you are right, for that is what I am. ¹⁴So if I, your Lord and Teacher, have washed your feet, you also ought to wash one another's feet. ¹⁵For I have set you an example, that you also should do as I have done to you. ¹⁶Very truly, I tell you, servants are not greater than their master, nor are messengers greater than the one who sent them. ¹⁷If you know these things, you are blessed if you do them. ¹⁸I am not speaking of all of you; I know whom I have chosen. But it is to fulfill the scripture, 'The one who ate my bread has lifted his heel against me.' ¹⁹I tell you this now, before it occurs, so that when it does occur, you may believe that I am he. ²⁰Very truly, I tell you, whoever receives one whom I send receives me; and whoever receives me receives him who sent me."

✴ ✴ ✴

The Unexpected Teaching:

Peter had to learn how to receive before he could learn how to give.

Much of what appears to be freely given actually costs a fortune. Many churches, for example, have encountered that wealthy member who puts a stout check in the offering plate every month but who also makes clear that if things aren't done her or his way, the church can kiss that money good-bye. During my college teaching days, I saw parents who generously offered to pay for a son's or daughter's education, provided the kid majored in something the parents approved of. And then there are folks who expect eternal love, acceptance, approval, gratitude, and loyalty as a result of a gift. In this case, the gift is an ever-present beam of sunlight, which the recipient should always remember and for which he or she should always be grateful. Any sign of disapproval of the giver is taken as disloyalty to one who has given so abundantly. Such gifts and givers just keep on taking.

There are, of course, more mundane examples. When I was around twelve years old, some friends and I saw an ad in the newspaper for a free case of Pepsi. Four hours later, after an excruciating demonstration of a Kirby vacuum cleaner, we had our Pepsi.

Then there's the guy who says, "Don't pay all that money to get your VCR cleaned; all it takes is some Q-Tips and alcohol. I'll do it for nothing." Six months later, when he tells you he can stop by to do that favor and you tell him you had it cleaned already, he's wounded and taken aback. His offer has now cost you a pile of awkwardness until you both forget about how ungrateful you've been.

Giving that isn't really free isn't giving at all. Strangely, only in receiving something absolutely free can one learn how to give freely. The unexpected component in Jesus' lesson for the disciples in this scriptural passage is that only by experiencing grace can one learn how to bestow grace. Peter and the others couldn't understand what it meant to give—not as the Kirby salesperson or the egotistical parishioner but as Jesus gave—until they knew what it meant to receive. They were told, "You also ought to wash one another's feet." They all needed to serve, but they also had to consent to be served.

One can tell by the way Peter received that he didn't yet know how to give. It's ironic, of course, that Jesus had to threaten Peter to get him to shut up and learn this lesson. In fact, Jesus' giving in the moment of this story had strings attached. Peter and his companions had to learn this lesson about giving and receiving if they were to feed and tend Jesus' sheep, as he called them to do in the closing chapter of John's Gospel. The giving and receiving Jesus modeled for the Twelve, and for us, was radical.

A couple of years ago, I was blessed to learn how powerful receiving can be. My mother had just come home from the hospital and was recovering from abdominal surgery. She was so weak she trembled. For a few weeks my sisters, brother, and I took turns caring for her, preparing her meals, bathing her, keeping her company. Allowing us to do this wasn't a matter of choice for Mom. She knew she couldn't do these things for herself, but it was uncomfortable for her at first. For years, Mom had felt terribly awkward about her body. But the time had come when necessity prevailed over modesty. Either her children would care for her, or strangers would have to. I'm grateful that she chose her children.

During the time I cared for Mom, I watched her spirit grow in peace and gentleness even as her body deteriorated. Tortured by years of powerful arthritis medicine, her body was practically falling apart. Her skin was so fragile that it bruised and tore with the slightest abrasion. In such a condition, she stood gaunt and shaky on a towel in front of her chair, and I washed her and put cream on her skin to ease its decay.

After a time of recuperation, Mom's health improved for a couple of months, and she was able to care for herself. But she was changed by the experience of receiving care. For one thing, there was a gentleness about her that's hard to put into words. When she gave hugs, she seemed somehow more present, more enduring and abiding and tender—not in some sappy way but in a sacred way. She was also aware of small blessings in a way that she hadn't been in the past. A ride in the car through neighborhoods to look at Christmas lights wasn't to be taken for granted anymore. The moments were holy. There was still pain, but there was also abundant grace, for her and those she loved.

I don't know for sure, but I'm betting that this is the grace that Jesus knew. He allowed Mary to anoint his feet with precious perfume. He allowed "a sinner" to bathe his feet with her tears, dry them with her hair, and anoint them with oil from her alabaster jar. He knew how and when to receive, and he called upon the Twelve—and he calls us now—to learn to do so as well. In receiving, we taste *agape,* God's unconditional love for us, and experience God's grace in Christ Jesus. And only then, from a full and grateful heart, can we give freely.

Invitation to Reflection

- ✘ When somebody offers you a compliment or thanks you, be aware of your impulse to minimize what you've been offered. The next time this happens, try simply saying, "You're welcome"—acknowledge the gift the other person is giving you, rather than refusing it.

- ✘ Ask yourself whether you are willing to let people do things for you. If not, what's uncomfortable about receiving? Is receiving an act of vulnerability?

- ✘ Is it possible to think of receiving as a way of giving to another person? Is receiving what people wish to offer you a way of hearing and validating them and their desire to reach out to others?

GOSPEL LOGIC

Mark 8:27–9:1

8 *²⁷Jesus went on with his disciples to the villages of Caesarea Philippi; and on the way he asked his disciples, "Who do people say that I am?" ²⁸And they answered him, "John the Baptist; and others, Elijah; and still others, one of the prophets." ²⁹He asked them, "But who do you say that I am?" Peter answered him, "You are the Messiah." ³⁰And he sternly ordered them not to tell anyone about him.*

³¹Then he began to teach them that the Son of Man must undergo great suffering, and be rejected by the elders, the chief priests, and the scribes, and be killed, and after three days rise again. ³²He said all this quite openly. And Peter took him aside and began to rebuke him. ³³But turning and looking at his disciples, he rebuked Peter and said, "Get behind me, Satan! For you are setting your mind not on divine things but on human things."

³⁴He called the crowd with his disciples, and said to them, "If any want to become my followers, let them deny themselves and take up their cross and follow me. 35 For those who want to save their life will lose it, and those who lose their life for my sake, and for the sake of the gospel, will save it. 36 For what will it profit them to gain the whole world and forfeit their life? 37 Indeed, what can they give in return for their life? 38 Those who are ashamed of me and of my words in this adulterous and sinful generation, of them the Son of Man will also be ashamed when he comes in the glory of his Father with the holy angels."

9 1 And he said to them, "Truly I tell you, there are some standing here who will not taste death until they see that the kingdom of God has come with power."

❦ ❦ ❦

THE UNEXPECTED TEACHING:
With Jesus, things were often backwards.

Jesus' disciples and other followers must have spent a lot of time feeling like bone brains. I get this impression when I read the Gospels and try to forget that, unlike Jesus' contemporaries, I already know Jesus' story and its details.

Take Peter. He correctly identified Jesus as the Messiah. He actually got something right. Then Jesus "sternly ordered" them all not to tell anyone about the news. A few minutes later, Jesus talked "quite openly" about how he was going to die. After reviewing the job description of the Messiah, Peter pulled Jesus aside to tell him something like, "Cut the death talk. You're the Messiah, remember?" Then Jesus said, "Satan, get the hell out of my way."

Now, if I were Peter, I'd be feeling a bit spacious between the ears. I was right about the Messiah, but then I was wrong about what exactly the Messiah was and what he was supposed to do.

Again, if I were Peter, I'd have to be thinking, *Look, if the Messiah's coming only to suffer, be rejected and killed, then what's the point of the whole Messiah thing anyway?* As for the "after three days rise again," I don't imagine I'd have even heard that part. I'd still have been back on "killed," especially now that I've left the fishing boat and followed Jesus. When I pretend I'm a disciple and try to understand what Jesus says and does, I get confused. All my assumptions about who God is and how God should operate keep getting crucified. This is what I like to call gospel logic. As a disciple, I think things ought to be done one way, and God says things should be done another way.

Example 1: Peter said, "Jesus, you're the Messiah. You have to live in order to bring in God's reign." Gospel logic: Jesus said, "You've got it backwards. I have to die to bring in God's reign."

Example 2: I say, "Jesus, I want to save my life." Gospel logic: Jesus says, "Then give your life to me."

Gospel logic is the operating principle of the life of discipleship. If I am to be a disciple, I have to accept that almost nothing is as I would expect it to be. The way I think just doesn't jibe with the way God operates, so either I'm off kilter or God is. After trying to live life on my own terms and failing repeatedly, I've decided that God's on kilter, and I'm off. The standards by which I used to measure contentment and meaning make a lot of sense, but they're actually nasty, gluttonous illusions.

As I write this meditation, I think of the Kennedy family, for example. I daresay that any Kennedy, in the midst of the many misfortunes those folks have suffered, would tell you that money's ability to control life is overrated. And all the billions in Bill Gates's computer fortune can't change that three-in-the-morning moment of wakefulness when folks look out the window at the moonlight and long to know the answers to questions that both rich and poor whisper into the darkness. No human skill or worldly renown can speak one meaningful syllable in response to a hunger for love never fed or a dream of intimacy never realized.

When I dupe myself into thinking that a new, faster computer will make my life significantly better, it's only a matter of time before gospel logic awakens me to the truth. The Spirit tries to teach me, through Scripture, my community, and experience, that I should seek out and live in God's will as best I can, even when that will appears contrary to common sense. Only by living in unity with my family of faith, reflecting on experience, and seeking wisdom and inspiration in the Bible can I begin to save my life.

Time and again, Scripture teaches gospel logic. God chose Sarah, "advanced in age" and way past menopause, to give birth to a people (Genesis 17–18). God chose Moses, "slow of speech and slow of tongue" (some scholars think he stuttered) and stubbornly reluctant to accept the position of ambassador to Pharaoh, to set God's people free from bondage in Egypt (Exodus 3–4). The resurrected Jesus chose to appear first to women and told them to share the good news of his living with the disciples—women, who probably wouldn't be believed

(Matthew 28; Luke 24; John 20). Christ chose Paul, a most zealous enemy of Christians, to build the church (Acts 9).

In short, everything's backwards, upside down. Children are wise, and the wise are foolish. The "poor in spirit" are given heaven, and the rich have to squeeze through the eye of a needle just to get in. Gospel logic!

To teach us how to live, God calls us to look upon how Jesus died. To teach us how to pray for healthy living, God calls us to listen to Jesus praying in Gethsemane before dying. To teach us how to forgive so we can get on with our lives, God shows us how Jesus forgave at Calvary so that he could get on with his dying. To teach us how to open our arms to all of the joys and blessings of life, Jesus opened his arms to the nails and humiliation of death. To teach us what's worth living for, God tells us what Jesus died for. Gospel logic!

Mike, a wonderful, gentle guy who taught me tai chi a few years ago, introduced me to gospel logic without realizing it. He was showing me a particular move I was struggling to master, and after letting me try to sort it out for myself, he asked me a question: "John, if you want to move to your left, what do you have to do first?"

"Uh," I said, "I don't know."

He said, "You have to move to your right first. That's tai chi logic. You think you should move to your left, but if you don't move to your right first, the move is impossible."

It's not worth trying to describe the move here, but in short order I discovered that Mike was right. I couldn't master the move, which had me going left, unless I first shifted my weight and leaned to the right—tai chi logic.

It's this way with gospel logic, too. I think I ought to move to my left, but God says, "Go right." This is the story of my life. I insist on going one way; God points out that I've got human things on my mind, not divine things. I'm being led by Coleman logic, not gospel logic. And so, like Peter, I find myself stunned, stung, and a little dazed. Then, for a few minutes, I try to make my way as best I can, moving backward, using the mirror God gives me to navigate, praying for the Spirit to give me the right steer when I'm foolish enough to suppose the gospel makes sense.

Invitation to Reflection

- Take some time to review your life. Are you now where you thought you'd be ten or twenty years ago? Has your life gone the way you thought it would?

- An old-fashioned but accurate way of thinking about gospel logic is in terms of rebellion against God, struggling against what the still, small voice of God might be trying to tell us. Are you aware of choices you've made in life that you now know were fighting against gospel logic?

- Where are you on your journey of openness to God's surprises and eccentricities? How have you grown? Where do you still have growing to do?

The (RE)VISIONARY

TEACHINGS

"The wind blows where it chooses,

and you hear the sound of it, but you do not

know where it comes from or where it goes.

So it is with everyone who is born of the

Spirit." (JOHN 3:8)

BROTHER JESUS?

Matthew 15:21–28

²¹*Jesus left that place and went away to the district of Tyre and Sidon.* ²²*Just then a Canaanite woman from that region came out and started shouting, "Have mercy on me, Lord, Son of David; my daughter is tormented by a demon."* ²³*But he did not answer her at all. And his disciples came and urged him, saying, "Send her away, for she keeps shouting after us."* ²⁴*He answered, "I was sent only to the lost sheep of the house of Israel."* ²⁵*But she came and knelt before him, saying, "Lord, help me."* ²⁶*He answered, "It is not fair to take the children's food and throw it to the dogs."* ²⁷*She said, "Yes, Lord, yet even the dogs eat the crumbs that fall from their masters' table."* ²⁸*Then Jesus answered her, "Woman, great is your faith! Let it be done for you as you wish." And her daughter was healed instantly.*

✽ ✽ ✽

The Unexpected Teaching:

Jesus changed his mind.

This teaching presents a struggle for me, and I'm betting the same is true for many other folks too. In this passage from Matthew, Jesus did something most human beings do every day—he changed his mind. Our temptation in reading the account of Jesus and the Canaanite woman is to say, "Oh, Jesus knew he was going to heal the Canaanite woman's daughter the whole time. He was just pushing the woman's buttons so that she would offer a full confession of faith in him." Unfortunately, Matthew doesn't tell us that Jesus had already discerned the woman's thoughts. The Gospel writers, especially John, never hesitate to tell us when Jesus had matters sized up beforehand. For example, in the exchange between Jesus and the Samaritan woman in John 4:1–43, Jesus lets the woman know (and us as well) that he knows her life circumstances before she reveals them to him. Because this story from Matthew offers no such indication, perhaps the Canaanite woman engaged Jesus in a fashion compelling or moving enough to get him to change his mind and widen his mission to include the Gentiles. Maybe he really didn't know what he was going to tell her ahead of time.

The safe path to take at this point would be to start talking about how wonderful it is that Jesus included all people—not just Israel—as worthy of his saving mission. Nope. Wonderful though that is, the unexpected issue raised here is Jesus' humanity, and it might do us all some good to consider this issue for a moment.

Jesus was human. This teaching is central to Christianity. The questions I lift up are, How human are we willing to let Jesus be? What does it mean to be a human being without sin? Is getting mad a sin, or is it simply unpleasant? Is changing one's mind sinful, or is it merely difficult for us to imagine Jesus doing so? To get a bit risky, is it sinful for a person to be conditioned by the culture in which he or she is raised? I realize these questions might be causing some discomfort, but certainly the act of asking questions is no sin.

Maybe my last question is best put aside for the moment. But we can look to Scripture for a clue about the sinfulness of changing one's mind. In Genesis 18, Abraham convinces God not to destroy Sodom if but ten righteous people live within the city. God had decided to level the place, but Abraham negotiated with God. So changing one's mind isn't a sin. Many readers also look at Genesis 32 and its story of Jacob wrestling with God at Peniel as an indication that humans are in conversation with God and that God really listens and responds.

How far can we push this point and still be faithful to our confession that Jesus the Christ is fully human, yet without sin? What's a sin, and what's just uncomfortable for us to accept? Jesus obviously got mad at the money changers in the temple, so getting angry, at least for the right reason, can't be a sin. And what about being troubled and afraid? When I read about Jesus praying in

Gethsemane, what I see is a person engaged in a significant struggle with feelings of terror. In Matthew's
Gospel, Jesus says, "I am deeply grieved, even to death"
(26:38)—sounds like sorrow and fear to me.

Pushing the envelope a bit further: Is it sinful to
grow up in a home where the parents teach that slavery
is a valid social institution, that women are subservient
to men, and that the needs of children are not all that
important? And is it sinful to be impacted by beliefs? We
have to be careful about how we answer such questions.
Lots of folks in Jesus' day, probably the majority, were
taught as I have just described. Were such beliefs inher-
ently sinful? Though slavery surely thrived in plain sight
of Jesus the man, he didn't speak out against it, at least
not that we know of. Yet he did clearly and forcefully
identify divorce, in many circumstances, as a sin (see
Matthew 5:31–32 and 19:9; Mark 10:11–12; and Luke
16:18). Despite such scriptural teachings, many of us
regard slavery's evil as a simple human truth and divorce's predominance as a regrettable but inevitable
human reality. Most people don't think of those who
oppress others as upstanding citizens, nor do they think
of divorced people as adulterers.

We could at this point fill our discussion with qual-
ifications. We might claim, for example, that slavery in
Jesus' day was an entirely different institution than it was
in the eighteenth- and nineteenth-century United States.
Or we could also say that divorce was more damaging
to Jesus' culture than it is to ours. But to take our thinking in this direction would be to distract ourselves. Our
purpose would be to protect Jesus from his own human-

ity. "Gosh," we would say, "slavery wasn't sinful back then. After all, people weren't sold into it. Lots of people sold themselves into slavery to improve their situations!" Then we would sit back, satisfied. Not that we care about whether slavery was evil in Jesus' day. We just want to keep him above the complex, sloppy fray of being human in a sinful world.

It can be threatening for us to see Jesus as a person who lived and ministered in a specific time and place. For one thing, God in Jesus the Christ becoming like us is just too much to swallow. For another, seeing Jesus as a person makes matters complicated for us. His humanity means we have to reflect continually on what his life and teachings are trying to tell us today in addition to what they tried to tell his contemporaries.

I'm willing to be convinced that I'm wrong about Jesus changing his mind in Matthew 15. I continue to struggle with the implications of my reading. In the end, however, I have a feeling that we contrive explanations for Jesus' human behavior in an effort to avoid accepting the cultural specificity of his teachings. At this moment in my journey of discernment, I sense Jesus calling us to think about how he would have us live now, not to accept uncritically teachings offered for particular reasons at particular moments. And this is frightening. Grace is frightening. When God takes on the flesh in Jesus, God calls us beyond neurotic haggling over rules to the task of being fully human, like Jesus of Nazareth was.

To follow rules mindlessly is to live as those whom Jesus scolded, the Pharisees. It is to live in fear of our own humanity. But to live as Jesus did, trying to understand what it means to be a faithful child of God, is to embrace both Jesus' humanity and our own. And so, like Jesus, we change our minds, get mad, and feel discouraged. We can do this because we know God did so too in the person of Jesus Christ.

Invitation to Reflection

✴ Call to mind the Jesus you believe in. Did Jesus really have to think about the decisions he made? Did he really listen to his friends and disciples, and was he willing to let them participate in decision making and wisdom seeking?

✴ What do we mean when we confess (as Christians do in the Nicene Creed), "For us and for our salvation he came down from heaven; by the power of the Holy Spirit he became incarnate from the virgin Mary, and was made [hu]man"? What does it mean for Jesus to be human?

✴ On a personal level, who is the Jesus of your faith? What kind of person is he? For example, is he "real folk"? Is he the sort of guy you could call brother? Would you sense in him the struggles all human beings endure, or would he not have to deal with the issues that confront other human beings?

POINT OF VIEW

Luke 10:25–37

25 Just then a lawyer stood up to test Jesus. "Teacher," he said, "what must I do to inherit eternal life?" 26 He said to him, "What is written in the law? What do you read there?" 27 He answered, "You shall love the Lord your God with all your heart, and with all your soul, and with all your strength; and with all your mind; and your neighbor as yourself." 28 And he said to him, "You have given the right answer; do this, and you will live."

29 But wanting to justify himself, he asked Jesus, "And who is my neighbor?" 30 Jesus replied, "A man was going down from Jerusalem to Jericho, and fell into the hands of robbers, who stripped him, beat him, and went away, leaving him half dead. 31 Now by chance a priest was going down that road; and when he saw him, he passed by on the other side. 32 So likewise a Levite, when he came to the place and saw him, passed by on the other side. 33 But a Samaritan while traveling came near him; and when he saw him, he was moved with pity. 34 He went to him and bandaged his wounds, having poured oil and wine on them. Then he put him on his own animal, brought him to an inn, and took care of him. 35 The next day he took out two denarii, gave them to the innkeeper, and said, 'Take care of him; and when I come back, I will repay you whatever more you spend.' 36 Which of these three, do you think, was a neighbor to the man who fell into the hands of the robbers?" 37 He said, "The one who showed him mercy." Jesus said to him, "Go and do likewise."

۲ ۲ ۲

THE UNEXPECTED TEACHING:
Who are you in this story?

I've lived my whole life as a middle-class citizen of the United States. I've gone to bed hungry but once in my life, and that was during a fast my church youth group organized. I've never had to worry about keeping a roof over my head. I was unemployed for about a year and went through some tough financial times, but I always knew somebody would take me in and feed me if I found myself out on the street.

Because of this fairly secure life I've led, I tend to read the parable of the Good Samaritan from the point of view of one of the three characters in the position to help out the guy in the ditch. Usually, I think of the priest or Levite and realize my own fearful impotence in reaching out to others in crisis or need. On rare occasions, I assume the role of the Samaritan, though even as I do so I'm aware that I don't give as much as that generous character did. It is telling, however, that I never see myself as the man who was robbed and beaten.

Jon Sobrino, Robert McAfee Brown, and other liberation theologians point out that much of the world, poor as it is, doesn't read the parable of the Good Samaritan as I do. Founded on the conviction that the gospel is at its heart the good news of freedom for folks experiencing every sort of oppression, liberation theology claims that God holds the poor and suffering in special love and concern. It also acknowledges that the way people read the Bible is undeniably influenced by the culture in which they find themselves.

Just as my middle-class situation affects my reading of this story, so too millions of Christians' impoverished existence leads them to step into a particular set of shoes (or sandals, as the case may be). Many poor or oppressed folks understand probably the most well-known story in the New Testament from the point of view of the man who was robbed and beaten.

There is something to learn from what the story says to the person in the ditch. Those of us who can afford to buy a book already know what the story says to us—being a priest or Levite means nothing if we switch sides of the road when we see someone in need. What we don't know so well is what the story can teach us if we acknowledge the perspective of a person who feels wounded and helpless, left for dead.

The first truth we might learn from this reading is what a helpless person needs, and here we're going to assume, taking our lead from liberation theologians, that the help offered by the Samaritan was insightful and effective. The Samaritan's actions demonstrated that generous, practical assistance was called for. He bandaged the man's wounds, gave him a ride to the inn, and took care of him. Then, before leaving the next day, the Samaritan picked up the tab and saw that the man got continued care. He assumed responsibility for the man's most basic needs until he was well enough to care for himself again.

Nowhere does it say that the Samaritan tried to get the wounded man to join his church or that he had any motive for helping whatsoever other than pity. I can anticipate the reply. "You dimwit," some might say, "we're also supposed to 'go therefore and make disciples of all nations, baptizing them in the name of the Father and of the Son and of the Holy Spirit, and teaching them to obey everything that I have commanded you'" (Matthew 28:19–20a, the Great Commission). In so doing, we reason, we bring people into the church—presumably our church.

Coupling what we might call the "mission" of the Samaritan with the Great Commission sounds like solid, practical theology. But taking that next subtle step—"I'll help you out; you get baptized; then join my church"—isn't faithful but opportunistic. Soup kitchens used to employ such theology: put food in front of somebody, but make them earn it by listening to preaching. The parable of the Good Samaritan teaches us that proclaiming the gospel to people lying wounded in a ditch, literally or figuratively, means to bind up their wounds and get them to safety. That's preaching the gospel in such a situation. Above the thermostat in my house, right where I'll see it a couple of times a day, I have a little laminated sign that reads, "Preach the Gospel. Use words if necessary" (Saint Francis of Assisi). In ministering to helpless people, no words are required. Just as God gives grace without strings, so we should offer aid without expectation of anything in return—even belief. Of course, there does come a time for words, but the Word happens in the context of relationships and community. The Good Samaritan's practical ministry *is* his proclamation. There can be no doubt that the wounded man was affected by the Samaritan's generosity and compassion. Maybe they even met again, and, in their relationship built on the foundation of radical kindness, the Samaritan had the opportunity to share his story of faith and, in turn, listen to the man he saved. I wonder if genuine sharing, which is to say any carrying out of the Great Commission, would be possible outside of a relationship established on the ground of grace.

I also wonder if the Samaritan could have acted as he did had he not been "moved with pity." As I try to put myself in the shoes of a person in a tough spot, I'm attracted to these three words. It's significant to note that the priest and Levite are not "moved with pity." Jesus could have easily told this story and made these two characters feel for the beaten man. I mean, why not say, "a priest was going down that road; and when he saw him, *he was moved with pity, but he feared robbers might still be near; so* he passed by on the other side" (italicized words my addition). But Jesus didn't tell the story that way. Only the Samaritan was "moved with pity."

The Samaritan's motivation for acting is not to be neglected. We don't know why the priest and Levite hustled past the scene of the crime, but we do know why the Samaritan stopped. There was in him a marriage of emotion and action. He cared about the man in the ditch and did something about it. The problem with this detail in the story is that there is no way to teach caring, at least no way that I know of. Nevertheless, what the story would have us understand is that faithfulness calls each of us to be the sort of person who is moved by the plight of others. Lying caked in my own blood, I imagine it would matter to me that someone might care about what I was going through. I would want to be loved.

The Samaritan's actions speak of love. He didn't blame the victim for his situation, didn't say, "Why did you walk alone on the road? Why were you carrying so much money?" He helped without judging the man's worthiness or ability to repay. And he didn't help halfway. He left a cash deposit and later picked up the whole tab. To be sure, there are situations when folks in need ought to work for the assistance they receive, but this wasn't one of them. The key is that the Samaritan's love wasn't based on whether the man deserved to be loved but that he was a human being in trouble. Merit wasn't the issue; grace was.

Were I in the ditch, the parable of the Good Samaritan would not only speak to me about what love means, but it would also let me know who I might be able to count on. And here, this reading of the story grabs me by the lapels. It isn't the pastors who are likely to give me a hand but a Samaritan, somebody who would be regarded by the wider religious community as heretical and unclean. Maybe I'm overstating matters here. Jesus' point was that the ability to do good isn't based on what titles come before people's names but what's in their hearts. Still, I suspect I would nod my head in recognition at the suggestion that those who ought to be most inclined to help often fail to do so.

The parable of the Good Samaritan, then, isn't one story but many. It's the story of a priest, a Levite, a Samaritan, a half-dead man, an innkeeper, and a lawyer who got sassy with Jesus and listened to a story. Particularly when we read the story from the point of view of the half-dead man, this is a parable of God's grace, given freely and abundantly, and for the sake of mercy alone.

Invitation to Reflection

⚹ Some of Jesus' most helpful and challenging teachings open up to us if only we can bring ourselves into awareness of who we are and what we're about. Who are you as a reader of the Bible? What beliefs, values, and attitudes are most central to your daily living?

⚹ How do these attitudes shape your reading of Scripture (and your engagement with everything and everybody, for that matter)?

⚹ How do your attitudes hinder you from loving in the fashion of the Good Samaritan?

The Wicked, the Gnarled, and the Wounded

Matthew 21:33–46

33 "Listen to another parable. There was a landowner who planted a vineyard, put a fence around it, dug a wine press in it, and built a watchtower. Then he leased it to tenants and went to another country. 34 When the harvest time had come, he sent his slaves to the tenants to collect his produce. 35 But the tenants seized his slaves and beat one, killed another, and stoned another. 36 Again he sent other slaves, more than the first; and they treated them in the same way. 37 Finally he sent his son to them, saying, 'They will respect my son.' 38 But when the tenants saw the son, they said to themselves, 'This is the heir; come, let us kill him and get his inheritance.' 39 So they seized him, threw him out of the vineyard, and killed him. 40 Now when the owner of the vineyard comes, what will he do to those ten-

ants?" 41 They said to him, "He will put those wretches to a miserable death, and lease the vineyard to other tenants who will give him the produce at the harvest time."

42 Jesus said to them, "Have you never read in the scriptures:

'The stone that the builders rejected
    has become the cornerstone;
this was the Lord's doing,
    and it is amazing in our eyes'?

43 Therefore I tell you, the kingdom of God will be taken away from you and given to a people that produces the fruits of the kingdom. 44 The one who falls on this stone will be broken to pieces; and it will crush anyone on whom it falls."

45 When the chief priests and the Pharisees heard his parables, they realized that he was speaking about them. 46 They wanted to arrest him, but they feared the crowds, because they regarded him as a prophet.

❧ ❧ ❧

THE UNEXPECTED TEACHING:
The chief priests and Pharisees knew
Jesus was the Messiah.

A brief summary of what happened immediately before this passage might be helpful. Jesus had just made his triumphal entry into Jerusalem, then had a tantrum in the temple and cleared the place of money changers and dove sellers. He cursed the fig tree, and now he was teaching in the temple. The chief priests and elders of the people were hassling him. First, they asked Jesus a question about baptism, but he frustrated their intent by tossing the question back at them. Then, he told the parable of the Two Sons, the moral of which was that the prostitutes and tax collectors were ahead of the religious authorities in the line into the kingdom of God. Finally, came the parable of the Wicked Tenants (Matthew 21:33–46).

So the setting for the telling of this parable was the temple, and the listeners were the chief priests, the elders of the people, and the Pharisees—the big boys. I used to think of these illustrious men as sincere but misguided. But a close reading of this parable presents a disturbing reality. Here, Jesus suggested that the tenants knew who the owner's son was when he showed up, and they killed him for that reason. If the tenants are to represent the big boys, then the claim here is that they persecuted and eventually killed Jesus because they knew he was the Messiah.

Actually, Matthew's overall portrayal of the religious officials is that they are beyond repentance. They simply can't tolerate goodness. They didn't want to destroy Jesus because they were mistaken about him. They didn't want to kill him because they viewed him as evil. They wanted to kill him because he was the Son of God. Even now, as I write about this, I just can't get it to sit right with me. For years, I guess I really didn't accept that there are now and always have been evil people in the world. I figured that people themselves weren't evil, but what they did might be. But Matthew teaches that some people are evil, and they react violently to what's good.

Although I'm in no position to say who is evil and who is good (especially because human beings are a combination of both), I have seen folks react quite negatively to good. A good example of this is some of the older, married, female students I used to teach in college. When writing essays for my English class, they often drew from their own experiences. Some of them wrote about, or talked to me about, the fact that their husbands were troubled by the education they were receiving. Wives got new ideas in their heads, and suddenly the household system was upset. Some husbands did all they could short of physical force to hinder their wives from getting a college education. One woman told me that her husband frequently asked why she bothered studying. She was stupid, he said. What good would college do her?

Now, I know few people who will say that education is a bad thing; in fact, most say it's good. Why, then, did these husbands get bent out of shape at their wives' efforts to learn and grow? They didn't want their happy home all fussed up by new ideas. The guys had a good system going and didn't want it threatened. They responded negatively to something good because it didn't suit their needs.

Another example of the same phenomenon, though on a more bloody scale, is the martyrdom of the religious in Central America over the past twenty or so years. Probably the most well-known martyr of that region is Archbishop Oscar Romero, who was shot while conducting Mass in 1980. Romero was appointed because many assumed he would be a Milquetoast, but instead he advocated for the poor and oppressed in El Salvador. This, of course, upset both church and governmental leaders. How dare Romero try to upset the comfortable lives of the rich and powerful by moving to address the staggering, grinding poverty and oppression of the masses? So they shot him dead at the Lord's Table.

It is hard to imagine that some Salvadoran leaders didn't know in their gnarled spirits that Romero and others who tried to help the poor were doing good. The problem is, nobody can fully uncover or understand the thoughts of another. All we know is that, by nearly every objective standard a reasonable person can come up with, the powerful in El Salvador reacted to this good with ruthless violence. We can observe, however, that steps to ease the poverty of the masses would at least take the luster off the lifestyles of the big boys. Obviously, they didn't give that reality a nice warm hug.

Jesus got pretty much the same response from the chief priests, the elders of the people, and the Pharisees that Romero got from Salvadoran leaders. We can't read the thoughts of the powerful, but we can say that Jesus perceived the hearts of folks with a bit more clarity than we do, and his teaching in the parable of the Wicked Tenants is that not only do some people react violently to good, they do so in the full awareness of their actions.

This teaching, though uncomfortable, does provide an odd, unexpected measure of comfort. Sometimes, we are mistaken when we believe we're doing good, and at such times we need to pull back and reflect on our own motivations. Other times, however, we're doing good, and we're met with resistance baffling in its zeal. At such moments, this parable is a helpful reality check. There is evil in the world, and from time to time, it wants nothing more than to crush good; moreover, such evil does sometimes act in full knowledge of its own hurtful nature.

Rarely do we have the wisdom to discern when we're dealing with evil of this kind. Even so, Matthew teaches us that it does exist. It's got fangs, and human wisdom can't always explain it away.

Invitation to Reflection ⚘

- ✘ Can you think of a situation in which a person is angry about something that should be good? How might that person be threatened by what ought to be good?

- ✘ The evil we most often come across isn't conscious, intentional evil. Generally, folks who act out are so wounded and confused that they can't see the good they're raging against. It's important to note that evil, whether it's purposeful or not, is to be met with compassion—which is not to say compliance. Think for a moment of a person who is hurting and lashing out at others. How might you respond with helpful, competent compassion?

- ✘ What might be a faithful response to what you perceive to be intentional evil?

DOING HEAVEN

Mark 10:13–27

13 People were bringing little children to him in order that he might touch them; and the disciples spoke sternly to them. 14 But when Jesus saw this, he was indignant and said to them, "Let the little children come to me; do not stop them; for it is to such as these that the kingdom of God belongs. 15 Truly I tell you, whoever does not receive the kingdom of God as a little child will never enter it." 16 And he took them up in his arms, laid his hands on them, and blessed them.

17 As he was setting out on a journey, a man ran up and knelt before him, and asked him, "Good Teacher, what must I do to inherit eternal life?" 18 Jesus said to him, "Why do you call me good? No one is good but God alone. 19 You know the commandments: 'You shall not murder; You shall not commit adultery; You shall not steal; You shall not bear false witness; You shall not defraud; Honor your father and mother.'" 20 He said to him, "Teacher, I have kept all these since my youth." 21 Jesus, looking at him, loved him and said, "You lack one thing; go, sell what you own, and give the money to the poor, and you will have treasure in heaven; then come, follow me." 22 When he heard this, he was shocked and went away grieving, for he had many possessions.

23 Then Jesus looked around and said to his disciples, "How hard it will be for those who have wealth to enter the kingdom of God!" 24 And the disciples were perplexed at these words. But Jesus said to them again, "Children, how hard it is to enter the kingdom of God! 25 It is easier for a camel to go through the eye of a needle than for someone who is rich to enter the kingdom of God." 26 They were greatly astounded and said to one another, "Then who can be saved?" 27 Jesus looked at them and said, "For mortals it is impossible, but not for God; for God all things are possible."

❦ ❦ ❦

THE UNEXPECTED TEACHING:
The kingdom of God is more than heaven.

In the verses preceding this scriptural passage, Jesus was being pestered about the specifics of the law. First, the Pharisees wanted to know Jesus' take on divorce. Then, his own disciples nagged him about it too. So both the Pharisees and the disciples were absorbed by trying to figure out the kingdom of God. They wanted to know what exactly was right and what was wrong. The law had to be perfectly clear, and if anything was vague, they felt like they had an itch in the middle of their backs they couldn't quite reach. It drove them nuts. For the Pharisees, their desire to torpedo Jesus added zest to the conversation.

When Jesus started to interact with the kids, it became clear immediately that the Pharisees and disciples just didn't get it. Rather than opening their eyes and seeing the kingdom of God when it greeted them, they just kept going after that itch in the middle of their backs—with a jackhammer.

But lest you think this is blowing spitballs at the Pharisees and disciples, remember that we're just like them. For most of my life, I assumed that the kingdom of God was heaven, as in where I hoped to go when I die. When I used to read "whoever does not receive the kingdom of God as a little child will never enter it," I thought, *I've got to figure out some way of having the simple belief of a child, or I'm going to the great barbecue.* When I read, "It is easier for a camel to go through the eye of the needle than for someone who is rich to enter the kingdom of God," I thought to myself, *Well, no big worries at the moment. I'm not rich. But if I do get rich, I'll try to learn to scrunch my hump way down.*

I know I'm not alone in thinking of the kingdom of God as the very last exit on Jesus' cosmic turnpike. But to view it this way is to look with only one eye—and that one only half open. In the New Testament, "the kingdom of God" also takes as its synonyms "the reign of God" and "the kingdom of heaven." In Hebrew, the concept is referred to as the *malkuth shamayim.*

Although there is no English equivalent, the closest translation would probably be "the reigning of God." The nuance is telling. What we often talk about as a place, the *kingdom of God,* is more appropriately thought of as the event of God's acting in the world. The kingdom of God, therefore, is both wherever and whenever the will of God is manifest in the hearts and actions of people. When the poor are fed and clothed, the kingdom of God is tangible. The living room in which a child is spoken to with love and respect is the reigning of God. So are the front porch on which two people in love really listen to each other and the office in which one colleague reaches out to another in a time of sorrow or despair. The *malkuth shamayim* is not just for the future; it's also for right now. Although we live with the promise that God's reign of justice and mercy will be complete when Jesus Christ returns (what theologians call the *eschaton*), we also exist in the present reality of this reign.

When we recognize God touching with our hands and speaking with our lips, we begin to see that Mark 10:13–27 isn't so much about what behaviors get us into a distant heaven but what behaviors constitute participation in the will of God. Heaven, then, is at least as much something we "do" as it is a place to which we go. Jesus tells us in this passage that a relentlessly anal-retentive mind isn't what the kingdom of God is about, and neither is a swollen bank account or investment portfolio. If we're constantly worried about what rules to follow or what stock to buy next, we lose sight of the open arms of Jesus, who is waiting to touch us and bless us, as he did the little children. Jesus surrounded by the little children is a reigning-of-God moment, not because they were kids but because he loved them and they accepted his love. I don't presume to oversimplify God's reign, but at its heart, I think, is this reality: the giving and receiving of love.

For adults and wealthy folks, it's tough to participate in the kingdom of God—wherever and whenever it blossoms. If one is fixated on the intricacies of the law or the trajectories of interest rates, one can't be focused on the radical love of God. We tend to think of Jesus' teaching in Mark 10 as a prediction for the dying. It is at least as much a prescription for the faithfulness and joy of the living.

Invitation to Reflection

- Where do you see the "reigning of God" (or heaven) present in your own life? How do you feel about heaven being present at this moment and awaiting us in the future?

- The poor, sick, grieving, and oppressed are sometimes told that they should simply endure their circumstances in this life and take comfort in the future coming of God's kingdom. How would an understanding of heaven as the present and future will of God challenge this bit of advice?

❦ If we understand the reigning of God as something we participate in—if, indeed, we "do heaven"—how do our attitudes toward our choices in this life change? Is it possible, for example, to ignore the cries of the poor and oppressed and "do heaven" at the same time?

JESUS THE CRIMINAL

Luke 23:26–43

^{26}*As they led him away, they seized a man, Simon of Cyrene, who was coming from the country, and they laid the cross on him, and made him carry it behind Jesus.* ^{27}*A great number of the people followed him, and among them were women who were beating their breasts and wailing for him.* ^{28}*But Jesus turned to them and said, "Daughters of Jerusalem, do not weep for me, but weep for yourselves and for your children.* ^{29}*For the days are surely coming when they will say, 'Blessed are the barren, and the wombs that never bore, and the breasts that never nursed.'* ^{30}*Then they will begin to say to the mountains, 'Fall on us'; and to the hills, 'Cover us.'* ^{31}*For if they do this when the wood is green, what will happen when it is dry?"*

^{32}*Two others also, who were criminals, were led away to be put to death with him.* ^{33}*When they came to the place that is called The Skull, they crucified Jesus there with the criminals, one on his right and one on his left.* ^{34}*Then Jesus said, "Father, forgive them; for they do not know what they are doing."* And *they cast lots to divide his clothing. 35 And the people stood by, watching; but the leaders scoffed at him, saying, "He saved others; let him save himself if he is the Messiah of God, his chosen one!" 36 The soldiers also mocked him, coming up and offering him sour wine, 37 and saying, "If you are the King of the Jews, save yourself!" 38 There was also an inscription over him, "This is the King of the Jews."*

39 One of the criminals who were hanged there kept deriding him and saying, "Are you not the Messiah? Save yourself and us!" 40 But the other rebuked him, saying, "Do you not fear God, since you are under the same sentence of condemnation? 41 And we indeed have been condemned justly, for we are getting what we deserve for our deeds, but this man has done nothing wrong." 42 Then he said, "Jesus, remember me when you come into your kingdom." 43 He replied, "Truly I tell you, today you will be with me in Paradise."

٭ ٭ ٭

THE UNEXPECTED TEACHING:
Jesus was executed as a criminal.

As a Christian, I say outrageous things just about every day. I eat the body and blood of Jesus when I participate in Holy Communion. I claim that Jesus rose from the dead. I hold on to the promise of eternal life, though I really have no empirical evidence that any life at all exists or will exist after physical death. Nevertheless, as Martin Luther suggests in his *Small Catechism*, the Holy Spirit calls me through the gospel to confess such crazy truths. Of course, I can't believe or confess anything on my own but rely on the Spirit to continue to call and inspire me to live according to a theology that sounds flaky to somebody from another faith tradition.

Strange as many Christian beliefs may sound, I love to confess them. Saying "Jesus rose from the dead, and so will I" feels liberating. But there are other realities of the faith that I generally ignore because they're disconcerting. One of the hardest to get my mind around is that Jesus was a criminal. My instinct is to temper Jesus' criminality immediately by saying, "Oh, he did nothing wrong. It was just a bunch of corrupt or evil or selfish or misguided men who had him tortured and killed. Jesus wasn't really a criminal."

But he was. Jesus claimed to have the authority to forgive sins. According to the law, this was blasphemy. Jesus also broke the law by picking grain and healing on the Sabbath. When he was brought before Caiaphas and Pilate, he offered them stony silence and what must have seemed to them evasive answers. Let's think honestly about how we would receive such a person as Jesus today. Let's call her Josephine. If Josephine taught wisely and with great insight, healed people of their illnesses, and told them that she forgave them for their sins, what would we do? If she were also silent or flippant when engaged by recognized religious leaders, then what would happen?

I doubt Josephine would be flogged and crucified, but you never know. More likely, she'd be ridiculed. We'd call her a kook, and the civil authorities would maybe keep an eye on her, lest we have another Heaven's Gate, Waco, or Jonestown on our hands. Josephine the miraculous healer would be dismissed as trickster or hustler. If we want to be honest, we have to ask, Would Jesus stand a chance with us?

I'm betting in our culture that Jesus would be considered a potentially dangerous weirdo we'd have to watch closely. In his own day, he was a formidable subversive. In calling into question the authority of religious and civil leaders and suggesting that laws were somewhat pliable in their application, he invited what must have felt like anarchy to many. His teachings threatened the stability of the culture. And that's what laws are for, to maintain stability.

People who threaten the existing power system in a society are criminals. Martin Luther King Jr. and Mahatma Gandhi both spent many a long hour in the clink. They were killed too. History, of course, has cleared both men of all the sorry charges against them and convicted their jailers, but that is now. This was then.

So I am putting the human Jesus in the same cell with King, Gandhi, Rosa Parks, Dietrich Bonhoeffer, Father Daniel Berrigan, and Nelson Mandela. Toss in your own prisoner of choice. No, I'm not trying to get Jesus dirty by sticking him in jail with these regular human beings, but I am trying to get a reality to sink in. Jesus lived and died as a dangerous criminal in the eyes of the authorities, and his status as criminal ought to mean something to me.

I understand that what I'm suggesting will be difficult for folks who think of Jesus, the law of the land, the Stars and Stripes, democracy, and the free enterprise system all as peas from the same pod. Saying that Jesus was a criminal—and therefore that God is a criminal too—has a heretical ring to it. But the fact is that Christianity is countercultural, that is to say, at least in some respects, criminal. Christianity goes against the norms, whatever they may be, because for the most part norms alienate and cause suffering. The word *normal* itself connotes acceptability. Christianity rejects this notion. If, for example, a society is wonderfully fair in its distribution of wealth but also normally oppresses women, then any Christian practice worthy of its name will take up women's concerns as its own. And if the economy of a society is thriving, but homosexuals are denied rights and regularly lashed to fence posts and beaten to death by good old, red-blooded heterosexuals, then Christians will reach out to homosexuals. In other words, it is those whom a nation would just as soon eliminate as look at that Christians should regard as God's and their greatest treasure. They are the ones the criminal Jesus came to gather into his arms.

Such is Jesus' brand of criminality, which teaches us that if we are to live as he would have us live, we ought to stand in solidarity with those whom society rejects, to call them sisters and brothers, to use whatever blessings we have that they might know the embrace of

Christ, and to find in them the presence of Christ waiting to teach and nourish us. And as I write elsewhere in these meditations, we should fully expect that our solidarity with society's rejects would brand us subversives and rejects. As disciples of Jesus, we'll destabilize our society and face persecution or at least make those around us uncomfortable because we won't mindlessly adopt the norms of our culture.

I'm aware that there's more than a pinch of idealism in what I'm saying here, but a less ambitious sensibility leads to complacency. Worse yet, rejecting the law-breaking Jesus of Scripture can lead only to rejecting the Jesus who comes to us in the angry environmental activist lying down before a bulldozer or the gay teenage couple walking hand-in-hand down the street.

Our challenge is to try to follow this Jesus who was executed between robbers, who comes to us still as criminal and outcast, who gives us strength should we find ourselves counted among subversives and rejects.

Invitation to Reflection

❧ I'll own up if you will: we try to make Jesus cuddly. The Gospels show a man who confronted nearly everybody with difficult—though ultimately liberating—truths. If Jesus had been as benign as we like to make him, who would have taken the trouble to nail him to a cross? Does your image of Jesus allow for a criminal element?

- In many families and churches, folks seem to place a high value on keeping the peace, on not rocking the boat. If we accept that Jesus had a decidedly rough edge to him, what impact might that have for how we relate to others in the home and the church? At what point should we place a priority on keeping peace? When should we risk conflict?

- What might the criminal Jesus say to us now in our social context? To what sorts of criminality might he call us? To what near and dear cultural values might Jesus object?

INCONSPICUOUS BRACKETS

John 7:53–8:11

[[7 *53 Then each of them went home,* 8 *¹ while Jesus went to the Mount of Olives. ² Early in the morning he came again to the temple. All the people came to him and he sat down and began to teach them. 3 The scribes and the Pharisees brought a woman who had been caught in adultery; and making her stand before all of them, 4 they said to him, "Teacher, this woman was caught in the very act of committing adultery. 5 Now in the law Moses commanded us to stone such women. Now what do you say?" 6 They said this to test him, so that they might have some charge to bring against him. Jesus bent down and wrote with his finger on the ground. 7 When they kept on questioning him, he straightened up and said to them, "Let anyone among you who is without sin be the first to throw a stone at her." 8 And once again he bent down and wrote on the ground. 9 When they heard it, they went away, one by one, beginning with the elders; and Jesus was left alone with the woman standing before him.* ¹⁰*Jesus straightened up and said to her, "Woman, where are they? Has no one condemned you?"* ¹¹*She said, "No one, sir." And Jesus said, "Neither do I condemn you. Go your way, and from now on do not sin again."]]*

❦ ❦ ❦

THE UNEXPECTED TEACHING:
One of the best-loved stories of Jesus is an addition.

In this meditation, the focus is not on the story itself but on the inconspicuous brackets. In many versions of the Bible, John 7:53–8:11 is presented between brackets, as it appears here. In my New Revised Standard Version, the footnote reads, "This account, omitted in many ancient manuscripts, appears to be an authentic incident in Jesus' ministry, though not belonging originally to John's Gospel." The New Jerusalem Bible has a footnote suggesting that the author of this passage was "possibly Luke." The New Living Translation tersely states, "The most ancient Greek manuscripts do not include John 7:53–8:11." The Novum Testamentum Graece (Greek New Testament), which most New Testament scholars use as the basis of their research, prints the text with a symbol denoting the following: "Enclosed words are known not to be part of the original text but printed because of the reading's great age or importance in the tradition."

The consensus among biblical scholars is that one of the best-loved stories of Jesus' ministry was not included in the oldest Greek manuscripts of John's Gospel but was added sometime later. A word of explanation might be in order for folks who have never heard about how the Bible comes to us in its present form. The oldest versions of the New Testament available to us were written in Greek, and very few of them are complete. Before the invention of the printing press, scribes—usually monks—made copies of Scripture in scriptoriums, where they wrote as others dictated to them in Greek. Numerous portions of the monks' handiwork are still in existence.

Scholars have developed methods for reading and examining these manuscripts, and what they've found can be a bit unsettling to some Christians. These scribes, often with the best and most faithful intentions, made changes in what they wrote. Sometimes, they misheard words and wrote them incorrectly. Occasionally, they wrote a note in the margin of the manuscript which, later on, was included as part of the text when the manuscript was copied again. And every once in a while, a scribe, working on his own from an original, made changes in passages that struck him as theologically flawed or inadequate.

In the case of John 7:53–8:11, it appears that at some point in time a copier of John's Gospel decided that this story of Jesus sticking up for the adulterous woman was too good to pass up. Now, unless we want to ignore all the hard work of scholars, we have to admit that the Gospel of John has something in it now that the original writer(s) didn't put there. Actually, the breadth of biblical research clearly shows that the process of translating and passing along Scripture is not only relentlessly human but also quirky. For example, one of the most valuable versions of the Greek New Testament in existence was discovered in the Near East at the Monastery of St. Catherine at Mount Sinai by Dr. Constantin von Tischendorf in 1844. He stumbled upon the manuscript, now called Sinaiticus, in a basket of papers to be used to light an oven. A monk told him that two baskets of such paper had already served as starter. Yikes! Because of serendipitous situations like this, not to mention the weathering effects of time, many manuscripts we now have in hand are missing significant portions. In short, the enterprise of piecing together our beloved Bible is sometimes simply the best guesswork of generations of researchers.

All this might be tough to accept, but it's the truth. The question is, What will we do with the fact that the story of Jesus standing up for the woman who committed adultery is an addition, most likely not part of the original Gospel of John? What will we do with the fact that there are scads of instances in Scripture of human beings adding to or otherwise changing the word of God? We Christians confess that Scripture is the divinely inspired word of God, but the processes described here don't sound very divine or inspired; in fact, it seems as though people have gotten their grubby handprints all over Scripture, goofing up a sentence here, copying a word down incorrectly there, adding a whole passage here. The Gospel of Mark has at least three different endings, depending on which ancient source one consults.

There are those who would dismiss everything I've written in this meditation and say, "Shoot, that guy just thinks about things too much. If it's in the Bible, that's good enough for me." My response is, "If it's in the Bible, that's good enough for me, too, but that's not where the discussion ends." I can't just pretend that there aren't eccentricities in the composition and compilation of Scripture. The fact that Mark's Gospel has at least three potential endings matters. It also matters that John 7:53–8:11 doesn't appear in the earliest manuscripts of that Gospel.

These realities affect the way we read all of Scripture. Because apparent mistakes in passing along the Bible were made over the centuries, because material got lost, because stories were added or deleted, we have to read that divinely inspired book with discernment and humility—and with largeness of vision. It is simply inadequate to read any single passage of Scripture, quote it with grit and determination, and consider the matter to which it speaks closed. We have to reflect on the whole of the Bible, prayerfully balance passage against passage, and take into consideration the context in which the words were written. And finally, we have to interpret all of Scripture in light of the life, death, and resurrection of Jesus Christ.

When we do these things, the issue of John 7:53–8:11 being added by some unknown person some centuries after the original was produced is not terribly pressing. Looking at the whole of Scripture, we see God nearly always working through goofy, neurotic, disobedient human beings. As we watch Jesus writing in the sand and calling the scribes and Pharisees to account for their own sinfulness, we might also remember him interacting with the rich young man or the Samaritan woman at the well, and we can say, "Yep, Jesus would've had mercy on a woman caught in adultery." When we consider the context of this story, we see Jesus being his good old radical self, sticking up for women like he always did. And when we look at the life, death, and resurrection of Jesus, we see once again in this story his grace and compassion, forgiving those who need forgiveness and confronting those who need a kick in the britches.

So we can accept the divinely inspired validity of John 7:53–8:11 and embrace its truth even though biblical scholars can't account for its factual authenticity. What matters isn't that the original author of John's Gospel wrote the story but that it echoes what we know of Jesus—his patient listening, bull's-eye insight, fearless commentary, and inscrutable character, which all of the brain power in creation can never explain or exhaust.

Invitation to Reflection

✘ As we learn new information, we sometimes need to reorient ourselves to new truths. How do the facts revealed in this meditation make you feel? As a result of reading this, will you need to revisit any of your opinions or beliefs about the Bible?

🗡 Many theologians remind us that the Bible is not to be worshiped for itself but to point to the One we worship. Can you think of ways that we might be guilty of worshiping the Bible rather than the God of whom it speaks? How might we be able to tell when this is happening?

🗡 Mark 2:27: "Then he said to them, 'The sabbath was made for humankind, and not humankind for the sabbath.'" Do you think it works to replace "Scriptures" for "sabbath" in this verse?

WEEDS AND
WHEAT TOGETHER

Matthew 13:24–43

24He put before them another parable: "The kingdom of heaven may be compared to someone who sowed good seed in his field; 25but while everybody was asleep, an enemy came and sowed weeds among the wheat, and then went away. 26So when the plants came up and bore grain, then the weeds appeared as well. 27And the slaves of the householder came and said to him, 'Master, did you not sow good seed in your field? Where, then, did these weeds come from?' 28He answered, 'An enemy has done this.' The slaves said to him, 'Then do you want us to go and gather them?' 29But he replied, 'No; for in gathering the weeds you would uproot the wheat along with them. 30Let both of them grow together until the harvest; and at harvest time I will tell the reapers, Collect the weeds first and bind them in bundles to be burned, but gather the wheat into my barn.'"

THE UNEXPECTED TEACHINGS OF JESUS

31He put before them another parable: "The kingdom of heaven is like a mustard seed that someone took and sowed in his field; 32 it is the smallest of all the seeds, but when it has grown it is the greatest of shrubs and becomes a tree, so that the birds of the air come and make nests in its branches."

33 He told them another parable: "The kingdom of heaven is like yeast that a woman took and mixed in with three measures of flour until all of it was leavened."

34Jesus told the crowds all these things in parables; without a parable he told them nothing. 35 This was to fulfill what had been spoken through the prophet:

"I will open my mouth to speak in parables;
I will proclaim what has been hidden from the foundation of the world."

36Then he left the crowds and went into the house. And his disciples approached him, saying, "Explain to us the parable of the weeds of the field." 37He answered, "The one who sows the good seed is the Son of Man; 38 the field is the world, and the good seed are the children of the kingdom; the weeds are the children of the evil one, 39 and the enemy who sowed them is the devil; the harvest is the end of the age, and the reapers are angels. 40Just as the weeds are collected and burned up with fire, so will it be at the end of the age. 41 The Son of Man will send his angels, and they will collect out of his kingdom all causes of sin and all evildoers, 42 and they will throw them into the furnace of fire, where there will be weeping and gnashing of teeth. 43 Then the righteous will shine like the sun in the kingdom of their Father. Let anyone with ears listen!"

✶ ✷ ✶

THE FIRST UNEXPECTED TEACHING:
Weeds and wheat were rooted together.

I admit to struggling a good bit to accept the parable of the Weeds of the Field. Jesus taught here that certain people were "sowed" by the devil, and that, at the end of the age, the angels will "collect out of his [the Son of Man's] kingdom all causes of sin and all evildoers, and they will throw them into the furnace of fire, where there will be weeping and gnashing of teeth." The suggestion was that some people were planted and raised by the devil, and I find this teaching difficult.

Lots of folks view the world in terms of easily discernable acts of good or evil and seem willing, maybe even eager, to accept that many people in this world will be damned to eternal torment. I know the "God hates fags" crowd really digs fire and weeping and gnashing. They seem to want front-row seats on such a spectacle.

I have several problems with so willingly consigning anybody to hell. First, although I've been moved by God's grace in my own life, I have little understanding of it. I barely know my own heart, let alone the hearts of others. Who am I to think I can say with any integrity who is forgiven and redeemed, and who is not? For that matter, who am I to question the efficacy of Jesus Christ's saving action to humanity in the first place? Second, Jesus specifically taught in the parable of the Weeds of the Field that the weeds were not to be pulled out by humans at all but by the angels. Apparently, we are not wise or discerning enough to know how to weed the field without killing all the good stuff. Third, and most to the point, the roots of the weeds were tangled up with the roots of the wheat. The image of roots is helpful for reflecting on the entanglement of good and evil. Above ground, where you can see what bears fruit, it's reasonably easy to tell what to harvest and what to yank. But even in daylight, one can't be sure about what's going on at the root level.

About ten years ago, my wife, Kathy, and I planted a wildflower garden behind our home. We dug up the ground, spread the seed mix around, lay a white-gravel border around the whole thing, and waited. For a long time, the growth that I checked on every day looked suspiciously like weeds to me. Eventually, we had a riot of color on our hands, but even then there were flowerless, weedy-looking mysteries sticking out from between the blossoms. The truth was, even when the garden was in bloom, I didn't really know which plants were the inhabitants and which were the intruders. Making matters worse, all the growth was woven together so that flowers had weeds connected to them.

That's the reality of good and evil in creation right now. I'm not wise enough to know what exactly God had in mind in the beginning or what the end times are going to look like, but here and now I see a garden that only God can weed. Good and evil are in a snarl, so much so that, as with my wildflower garden, I sometimes can't tell which is which. Here are two examples. About four or five years ago, a neighbor down the street was caught fondling children. He was an upstanding citizen in town, beloved, it seemed, by all who knew him.

When he was brought to sentencing, friends and associates lined up to speak on his behalf. He ended up going to jail, where he may still be. So was this "weed" planted by the devil and destined to make his neighborhood radioactive? Or was he "wheat" planted by God and contaminated by Chernobyl? Was he the flower everybody loved or the weed that strangled young flowers?

Another example: an acquaintance of mine was bad news while growing up and even into adulthood. Many who knew the violence he brought upon others feared him. In prison, he had a reputation as someone not to mess with. To somebody who had seen him then, there could have been little doubt of his weedy nature. But then, as the years passed, he (and God) put his life in order, and he worked tirelessly for peace among feuding inner-city gangs. He is now a husband and father and in high demand as a speaker about his experience organizing a nationwide gang summit. Was he wheat that got poisoned? A weed that got transformed? Had he been "pulled" in his early years, kids alive today would have died in the gang wars he helped to prevent.

If the wheat and weeds metaphor can stand for actions as well as people, then the matter gets more complicated yet. In the movie *The Elephant Man*, Frederick Treves, the character played by Anthony Hopkins, gives the title character, John Merrick, a comfortable place to stay and good medical care. As their relationship develops, Treves wonders why he is being so helpful to Merrick. Is it to rescue a suffering, deformed man from a life of degradation or to make a name for himself in London society? Sitting up in the middle of the night, he asks his wife, who has come to check on him, "Am I a good man? Or am I a bad man?"

Why do we do the good or bad things we do? Do we help others so that we will be recognized? Do we hurt others because we have been hurt ourselves? For what are we to blame? And for what may we be excused? We are at once saints and sinners who keep getting tangled up in mixed motives.

In the parable of the Weeds of the Field, Jesus calls us to leave our confusion behind. Our job isn't to sort out good and evil. All we can do is accept God's grace and do our best to be wheat and not weed. We also have to accept the fact that there is evil in the world, evil that we don't understand, evil that sometimes looks suspiciously like good, evil that sometimes has an inexplicable capacity for redemption.

And so we pray out of faith, out of humility, to live lovingly and responsibly in the field.

THE SECOND UNEXPECTED TEACHING:

Jesus taught the crowds only in parables.

Let me state directly how confusing it is that Jesus taught the crowds nothing "without a parable." Even so, there's an important teaching to observe even in this confusion. Before I started reading the Bible closely, I lumped all of Jesus' followers together. I figured that whenever he opened his mouth, a jillion people were standing around listening, but this wasn't the case at all. What Jesus did was address the crowds in parables, but he went into more detail and straight talk with his disciples. Sometimes other folks—the crowds—overheard him teaching his disciples, yet Jesus told the crowds only parables. A good example of what I'm talking about is the Sermon on the Mount (Matthew 5:1–7:27). Here's how it opens: "When Jesus saw the crowds, he went up the mountain; and after he sat down, his disciples came to him. Then he began to speak, and taught them, saying . . ." So the most famous teaching in the New Testament was actually given to the disciples, apart from the crowd, which presumably overheard it.

What are we do to with the fact that in Matthew, Mark (4:10), and Luke (8:10), specific reference is made to Jesus teaching the crowds only in parables? Lots of people don't learn very well by hearing a story. Some need simple explanations. Why wasn't Jesus just as clear as possible with everybody? There's no way to know. Maybe lessons need to be earned, not given. Maybe reflecting on a parable permits the hearer to own the lesson in a way that a fully accessible delivery wouldn't.

There is, however, a distinction made between the disciples and the crowds, and this realization may open a few doors to meaningful thought and prayer. It is in this spirit—thought, prayer, faithful speculation—that I want to fuss with what the distinction between disciples and crowd might mean.

The first implication is that Jesus did not expect the same level of knowledge or commitment of everyone. He called people to different vocations in the life of faith. He called some, like the disciples, to leave everything behind and follow him, and he invited others to follow him in a different way. The immediate temptation is to suggest that the life to which disciples were called was more sacred, valid, or valuable than that of folks in the crowd. The problem with this impulse is that the nature of the calling was not in the person called but in the one who called. According to Mark 4:12, Jesus spoke to the crowd in parables "in order that 'they may indeed look, but not perceive, and may indeed listen, but not understand; so that they may not turn again and be forgiven.'" Nowhere did Jesus say that the disciples were any better than the crowd; in fact, we may presume that when Jesus did not explain the parables to the disciples, they were just as lost as the crowd. Their discipleship, therefore, was not a validation of their wisdom or maturity but a gift from God.

Nevertheless, a distinction was made. Some people were given greater understanding and insight than others. Maybe *some* isn't the right word; *precious few* is more like it. Unfortunately, we professional religious people want to monopolize the disciple role. "I have the insight," we say. "I thank God for the gift of understanding I've received" (and try to look convincingly humble). But there's a wrinkle in that assumption. If, as I wrote in the first section of this meditation, we don't have the wisdom to discern fully good and evil, we certainly can't claim to have our ears tuned to the Spirit more than anybody else.

The unexpected teachings of these parables in Matthew add up to humility. It's not anybody's role to sort out good people from bad people. Our powers of discernment aren't worthy of that angelic task. And we know what the parables mean only because Jesus explained them to us in Scripture; in a way, we can claim only to overhear what he said to his disciples.

In the end, I do feel called, like the disciples, to leave my boat and catch of fish on the beach, and I view that calling as a gift. Even so, like many in the crowd, I find myself in that field of people bending to hear the words of Jesus, sometimes catching bits of wisdom, often hearing only fragments, always hoping to be wheat and not weed, and always dependent on the breath of Jesus Christ for life and growth.

Invitation to Reflection

ж The parable of the Weeds of the Field raises the question: If God our creator is good, then where does evil come from? Matthew 13 indicates that "an enemy" introduced evil into a good creation, and now good and evil are tangled up with each other. Can you think of situations in your life, or in the lives of people you know, in which good and evil are bound together at the roots?

- Based on your experience, is it possible to say why rooting out evil will pull up good as well? Have you found this to be true?

- Because there are but few disciples and many in the crowd, we all have to prayerfully discern the particular vocation to which Jesus calls us. Take a moment to reflect on your vocation as a child of God. How do you understand, and how would you describe, your calling?

BEYOND MIRACLES

John 3:1–21

¹Now there was a Pharisee named Nicodemus, a leader of the Jews. ²He came to Jesus by night and said to him, "Rabbi, we know that you are a teacher who has come from God; for no one can do these signs that you do apart from the presence of God." ³Jesus answered him, "Very truly, I tell you, no one can see the kingdom of God without being born from above." ⁴Nicodemus said to him, "How can anyone be born after having grown old? Can one enter a second time into the mother's womb and be born?" ⁵Jesus answered, "Very truly, I tell you, no one can enter the kingdom of God without being born of water and Spirit. ⁶What is born of the flesh is flesh, and what is born of the Spirit is spirit. ⁷Do not be astonished that I said to you, 'You must be born from above.' ⁸The wind blows where it chooses, and you hear the sound of it, but you do not know where it comes from or where it goes. So it is with everyone who is born of the Spirit." 9 Nicodemus said to him, "How can these things be?" 10 Jesus answered him, "Are you a teacher of Israel, and yet you do not understand these things?

11 "Very truly, I tell you, we speak of what we know and testify to what we have seen; yet you do not receive our testimony. 12 If I have told you about earthly things and you do not believe, how can you believe if I tell you about heavenly things? 13 No one has ascended into heaven except the one who descended from heaven, the Son of Man. 14 And just as Moses lifted up the serpent in the wilderness, so must the Son of Man be lifted up, 15 that whoever believes in him may have eternal life.

16 "For God so loved the world that he gave his only Son, so that everyone who believes in him may not perish but may have eternal life.

17 "Indeed, God did not send the Son into the world to condemn the world, but in order that the world might be saved through him. 18 Those who believe in him are not condemned; but those who do not believe are condemned already, because they have not believed in the name of the only Son of God. 19 And this is the judgment, that the light has come into the world, and people loved darkness rather than light because their deeds were evil. 20 For all who do evil hate the light and do not come to the light, so that their deeds may not be exposed. 21 But those who do what is true come to the light, so that it may be clearly seen that their deeds have been done in God."

✻ ✻ ✻

The Unexpected Teaching:

Jesus asked Nicodemus to believe in something more than miracles.

One of the great things about Jesus is that he was always intellectually one step ahead of those around him. For this reason, Jesus sometimes appeared to come out with non sequiturs. In such situations, he was actually responding not to what folks said but to the foundation upon which their words were built.

The opening exchange between Nicodemus and Jesus is a good example of such an apparent non sequitur. Nicodemus, the Pharisee who was convinced that Jesus had come from God and who eventually helped prepare his body for burial, snuck to Jesus' lodgings under cover of darkness and said, probably in a whisper, that he believed that Jesus had been sent by God because of the miracles Jesus had performed. We should probably expect Jesus to say, "Come on in. Welcome aboard." Of course, Jesus didn't say this, because he heard not the other man's statement but the assumption upon which it was built: I believe in you, Jesus, because of your neat tricks. Can I be one of your followers and reap the rewards of being with you? And by the way, don't tell anyone I've been here.

Jesus didn't need to have his ego stroked, so he moved right past the compliment and addressed the real issue: "Nicodemus, the physical healing is really beside the point. I'm here to heal the wholeness of my people. If you're going to believe in me, you're going to have to get past the little miracles to the big one. Giving sight to the blind is only a pleasant residue of eternal life in my spirit."

Late in his conversation with Nicodemus, Jesus, who always seemed as concerned with people's motivations as their actions, returned to the issue of deeds and pulled an interesting reversal on his listener. Whereas in the beginning of the account Jesus suggested that belief needs to be based not on physical evidence but on spiritual rebirth, he used Nicodemus's own logic to indict the Pharisee himself: "all who do evil hate the light and do not come to the light, so that their deeds may not be exposed." Although in the Gospels Jesus repeatedly told people not to base their judgments of him on his marvelous actions, he was not above suggesting that evil actions were evidence of an evil identity.

When Nicodemus left Jesus' lodgings, therefore, he might not have fully understood what hit him. I see the lesson going something like this:

> "Nicodemus, you've shown up here at night and told me that you believe in me because of the signs I've performed. If you want to follow me, you need to believe spiritually that I'm sent from God.
>
> "If you're confused now, boy, are we in trouble. You're a teacher of the faith, and you're having trouble with what I'm saying. How can you teach others?
>
> "Nicodemus, God sent me into the world to perform miracles even bigger than the ones you can see. I'm here to give everlasting life. So you

see, judging me by my works is missing the forest for the trees.

"People who understand and accept what I'm saying here are in good shape. People who don't are condemned because they don't get it. Salvation is about much more than giving sight to the blind eyes. It's about giving eternal light.

"I can tell that people aren't understanding my message because they're doing lousy things—like sneaking around at night for fear of what others might think.

"If you want life in my spirit, you'd better come to me in daylight. And don't come to the back door. Walk right up to the front so everybody can see what you're doing."

The applications for living in this account are staggering. First, belief based on physical signs is faulty. Let's say you're terribly ill, and dozens of your friends pray for your healing. The next thing you know, wham, you're all better. The doctors can't believe it. "It's a miracle," they say. "We've never seen anything like it."

It may be that Jesus would like you to celebrate, but such a miracle should have no bearing on your faith. Jesus could love somebody just as much as he loves you, and that person might die a painful death—despite the church prayer chain doing hours of overtime. Does that mean Jesus doesn't exist? No. It must mean that physical healing does not indicate the entirety of Jesus' love for us. Physical healing might occur, but our whole human condition is what he really cares about. The health of our bodies is important, but so is the health of our minds and spirits.

Of course, the answering of prayers is a mystery. Why are some prayer requests apparently granted and others denied? Maybe it's because, like Nicodemus, we don't really hear what we're praying for, but Jesus does. He skips over the nonsense of our shopping-list prayers and addresses the foundation of our need, which is almost always something beyond our asking.

The point of Nicodemus's story is that the rebirth Jesus speaks of is a gift to which we must open ourselves. Like the wind, it comes from unexpected directions. It's unpredictable. It's a mystery! The only way to enter into it is to give one's self to Jesus entirely, to give up even the expectation of physical healing, even as we pray for it. If healing happens, wonderful, but it's still only a small sign of a larger reality: the touch of the one through whom the world is saved.

Invitation to Reflection

✶ What is your experience with God answering prayer? Are there times you can remember when God apparently heard a prayer that you didn't have the wisdom to utter and answered it?

✶ Systematic theologian Michael Root once said that prayer is our participation in the divine conversation. How would you describe your current understanding and practice of prayer? Any healthy conversation contains silence, as one person listens to another. Is there listening in your prayer? In what ways, if any, do you sense God speaking to you in prayer?

✎ I confess that, like Nicodemus and perhaps most of us, I would be very much drawn to a person who was performing miracles. But this brings up a poignant question: On what do we base our faith? How have you felt when you sensed that God wasn't hearing your prayer? What sense did you make of the experience? If you've experienced the miraculous, what impact did that have on your faith journey?

The SHALOM

TEACHINGS

"Now Simon's mother-in-law was in bed with a fever, and they told him about her at once. He came and took her by the hand and lifted her up. Then the fever left her, and she began to serve them." (MARK 1:30–31)

BINDING AND
LOOSING

Matthew 18:15–20

¹⁵"If another member of the church sins against you, go and point out the fault when the two of you are alone. If the member listens to you, you have regained that one. ¹⁶But if you are not listened to, take one or two others along with you, so that every word may be confirmed by the evidence of two or three witnesses. ¹⁷If the member refuses to listen to them, tell it to the church; and if the offender refuses to listen even to the church, let such a one be to you as a Gentile and a tax collector. ¹⁸Truly I tell you, whatever you bind on earth will be bound in heaven, and whatever you loose on earth will be loosed in heaven. ¹⁹Again, truly I tell you, if two of you agree on earth about anything you ask, it will be done for you by my Father in heaven. ²⁰For where two or three are gathered in my name, I am there among them."

❧ ❧ ❧

THE UNEXPECTED TEACHING:

The church was called to bind and loose people from the law.

I don't know many people who have read the Bible cover to cover and tried to understand it as a whole. I suppose this is because the Bible's such a fat book with skinny pages; the idea of reading it all is daunting. Many of us hear little chunks of it on Sundays, and some read a passage or two as part of daily devotions. The problem with this arrangement is that we sometimes take teachings out of context.

Matthew 18:15–20 is a good example of this phenomenon. This passage is frequently used in churches as a guide for dealing with people who act out, making life difficult and painful for others. Follow the process outlined in these verses, and—so the thinking goes—you can get rid of a pain in the neck from the church community and still call yourself a Christian in the morning. Unfortunately, there are a couple of problems with this approach. First, the passages before and after this one speak of the remarkable lengths to which believers should go to maintain a relationship with one who is lost. In Matthew 18:10–14, Jesus lifted up the shepherd who left ninety-nine sheep behind to find one that was lost. And in Matthew 18:21–22, Jesus told Peter that he should forgive another member of the church who sins against him, even seventy-seven times. The point here is that the famous disciplinary passage is part of a larger teaching that asks believers to go to nearly impossible lengths to keep these people a part of the community of faith, not give them the boot. The second problem concerns how believers should regard those who "refuse to listen even to the church." They are to be to the community of faith as "a Gentile and a tax collector." Many of us read that and say, "Gentiles and tax collectors! Ptew! Get 'em out of here!" Well, not exactly. In the Gospel of Matthew, Gentiles and tax collectors aren't presented as people the church should reject but as those the church should especially pursue in hopes of bringing them into (or back into) the community. When we read this passage as a way of getting rid of troublemakers, we're reading it plain wrong. Its purpose is to show how to keep people on board, not how to make them walk the gangplank.

This is just one example of how a piece of Scripture can get misused because we're not paying attention to context. Probably the most damaging misuse of Scripture occurs when folks quote specific references to "the law" as a way of identifying inappropriate behavior. And of course, if you want to be careless with the Bible, this is easy enough to do. Look hard enough and you can find a passage to support an assertion that almost anything is either wrong or right. A good example of this reality concerns the issue of homosexuality. Those who want to say that homosexuality is wrong and sinful can cite half a dozen or so verses, among them Leviticus 20:13: "If a man lies with a male as with a woman, both of them have committed an abomination; they shall be put to death; their blood is upon them." "Take that!" says the person who thinks homosexuality is bad. The person who thinks homosexuality is OK counters with Galatians 3:28: "There is no longer Jew or Greek, there is no longer slave or free, there is no longer male and female; for all of you are one in Christ Jesus." Gotcha!

And so the debate goes on ad infinitum, with folks flinging verses at each other like snowballs. The whole process is a colossal begging of the question. Each claim is, in fact, a question. When a person says that a behavior is wrong (or right) and whips a Bible verse at our heads, what he or she has done is not ended a discussion but begun one.

The issue here is whether a law is binding in a particular situation. Figuring that out first requires not just that we apply the law but that we understand how it is stated, its context, and its applicability to specific cases. It is the job of communities of faith to answer such questions, to discern the right answers, not to fling Bible verses at each other in order to exclude others from the church. Binding and loosing, as Matthew tells us, is the principle behind this process.

The original readers of Matthew well understood binding and loosing. New Testament scholar Mark Allan Powell writes, "In the historical setting for this Gospel, the terms 'bind' and 'loose' were used in rabbinic interpretations of the law to designate whether or not a specific scriptural admonition was applicable for a given circumstance." And in rabbinic tradition, Jesus did just this in all the Gospels. John 8:1–11 presents a good example of the spirit of Jesus' instruction to his disciples to bind and loose people from the law. The scribes and the Pharisees brought to Jesus a woman "caught in the very act of committing adultery." They told him, "Now in the law Moses commanded us to stone such a woman. Now what do you say?" After his inscrutable few moments of writing on the ground, Jesus said, "Let anyone among you who is without sin be the first to throw a stone at her." Jesus didn't say that the woman's adultery was appropriate; rather, he implied that the law in this particular case should not be enforced—perhaps because the scribes and Pharisees were in their own way as much in violation of the law as the woman was. In any case, Jesus "loosed" the woman from the law. He didn't enforce it. In Matthew 18:18, Jesus calls the church to this same task of discerning and applying the law.

Even given this call, it's interesting to note not only our Christian preoccupation with the law but the shape of Jesus' approach to the law in the Gospels. Somebody was always pestering him about rules, and Jesus continued to point beyond them. Rules can make life seem simple and easy, but we can't let ourselves forget that for Jesus, the needs of individuals and the community consistently took precedence over the law. It was simply more important to Jesus that people lived within the reign of a loving and merciful God than that they were able to keep the law.

And this is why the church is called to a task that takes precedence over binding and loosing. The Christian's first thought is of proclaiming in word and deed the saving action of Jesus Christ, who removed from our hearts and minds the burden of the law. In so doing, we look not upon our own weakness but upon the radical beauty of Jesus. The idea here is that we're so wrapped up in the love of Christ and so busy acting out this love to those around us that we're free of the anxiety and failure associated with keeping the law. We're not neurotically folded in on ourselves about it anymore. And when we do think about following the specifics of the law, we do so out of love for God and a desire to please God, not out of fear that disobedience makes us any less a child of God or leads to endless torment. So we try always to see obedience to the law through grace-colored lenses.

But here's where things get muddled. Often, we are unable to accept our freedom and find ourselves engaged in red-faced, eyeball-bulging debates over the law. And sometimes we can't help it. Should a person twice convicted of embezzlement be the church treasurer? Well, probably not. Should a pedophile be a pastor? Nope. A patina of sin covers the world. Although we know that grace alone puts us right with God, the process of living in community compels us to consult the law.

The question is, How do we as groups and individuals faithfully execute the task of consulting the law? How should we talk about the law? How should we use it? How should we be guided by it? Frankly, there are a lot more questions about the law than there are answers; nevertheless, a few guidelines are helpful.

First, we have to admit that our use of the law is uneven at best and shaped by our culture. We cannot follow the law objectively because our human frailty gets in the way all the time. Two examples demonstrate this point: slavery and money lending. Scripture raises no specific objections to the institution of slavery and in some cases even appears to condone it. What's more,

Scripture time and again clearly speaks out against the practice of lending money and charging interest. Nobody I know thinks it is in harmony with God's will to enslave folks or send bankers to the slammer. The realities of our culture lead us to bind or loose ourselves from the law, and we ought to admit that we do so erratically.

Second, we should also acknowledge that sometimes we're not even sure what the laws of Scripture are intended to address. For many a long year, the instruction of Ephesians 5:22 ("Wives, be subject to your husbands as you are to the Lord") was used to keep women in abusive relationships. Somewhere along the line, many in the church figured out that this admonition couldn't apply to physically or verbally violent situations—and even if it did, we reasoned that the needs of an abused woman were more pressing than a husband's need to be obeyed. When we talk about the law, then, it should always be with some humility about our own understanding of its intention.

And third, any use of the law that does not help a person to understand God's grace is unfaithful. The law should not drive people away from God but lead them to see their own and everyone's dependence on God for worth and health. A gay friend of mine once confessed to me in tears that he hated himself and thought God hated him too because he was unnatural. Whoever made him feel this way was wrong. The law isn't a set of rules that we're supposed to follow; rather, in Christ, it helps us to recognize the fragility and woundedness of every human being. The law helps us to understand how we all wish for connection with God and each other, how often we feel abandoned, how consistently we can't manage to do what we know is right, how predictably we do exactly that we know is wrong, and how, in fear and sadness, we respond to our disappointment and failures. If we talk about the law appropriately, we should find ourselves running into God's embrace.

Waving fists in each other's faces and spitting out a few Bible verses are misuses of the law. What we do instead, for our individual and communal health, is bind the law to and loose it from one another, binding it lovingly to help folks to see the reality of their relationship with God and loosing it to free those who have fallen into despair. And so we live in a constant process of discernment, seeking to know and do God's will in the context of grace and the law.

Invitation to Reflection

- There is tension between accepting God's grace and wanting to be guided by laws that make life manageable, and there's ambiguity in figuring out as faithfully as we can when to observe the law and when to move beyond it. How would you describe your comfort level in situations in which there are no clear solutions to problems or no immediate answers to questions?

- *The Oxford Companion to the Bible* records that "the Hebrew Bible has no term exactly equivalent to the English word 'law.' The Hebrew word most often translated as 'law,' *tora* (Torah), actually means teaching or instruction." How might this nuancing in translation affect the way we think of the law? What might it mean to think of biblical laws as teachings or instructions? What are the connotations of the words *law, teaching,* and *instruction?*

꙰ Can you think of a specific situation in which biblical law as you understand it seemed like it was not in harmony with the will of God? What was it about the law in that situation that did not reflect God's will?

BLESSING BLOSSOMS

Mark 1:29–34

29As soon as they left the synagogue, they entered the house of Simon and Andrew, with James and John. 30Now Simon's mother-in-law was in bed with a fever, and they told him about her at once. 31He came and took her by the hand and lifted her up. Then the fever left her, and she began to serve them.

32That evening, at sundown, they brought to him all who were sick or possessed with demons. 33And the whole city was gathered around the door. 34And he cured many who were sick with various diseases, and cast out many demons; and he would not permit the demons to speak, because they knew him.

❦ ❦ ❦

THE UNEXPECTED TEACHING:

*Simon's mother-in-law turned her blessing
into service.*

I can see how a woman reading this story of healing might feel annoyed. Simon's mother-in-law (the poor
woman didn't even get a name) was flat on her back with
a fever. Jesus and the boys showed up; Jesus healed her;
and she got up to fetch beer and ox roast sandwiches.
No chance to freshen up or anything. At least that's the
picture that comes to mind. We can't deny that Jesus of
Nazareth lived in a patriarchal society; nevertheless, if
we can put that point on the shelf for a moment, we can
find an unexpected teaching in this account for both gen-
ders and all races: the faithful response to God's blessings is service.

Blessings can come in the form of healing, but we
all know that there are lots of other ways people can be
blessed. Talents (for example, connecting with kids,
woodworking, singing, organizing, putting folks at ease)
are blessings—cultivated by hard work, no doubt, but
blessings all the same. Financial wealth is a blessing. So
is physical strength. So is a joyful spirit or a patient heart.

Sometimes, I fall into the trap of taking my blessings and running. For a lot of years, I used my writing
ability only for my own amusement or benefit. I published my work for the sake of recognition and financial
reward. (Trust me, I wasn't a big winner in either arena,
nor did I deserve to be.) I will say that I did try to create works that had some beauty or insight, and in this

regard what I did was worthwhile. The main reason I wrote, however, was that I wanted to be somebody. My estimation of my own worth was tied to how many poems I could publish.

And publish I did, a fair little pile of works mostly in literary journals, but in the meantime I died inside because I somehow knew that publications don't make a person valuable. Only when I discovered that my worth didn't depend on my own accomplishments but on the merits of Jesus Christ did I begin to live again, or maybe I should say that only then did I begin to live, period. And only then did I realize that writing would bring me the greatest joy not when I looked good because of it but when through it, with the Spirit's help, others would somehow feel closer to God.

Still, this world makes all of us, myself included, ravenous. Even in the midst of grace upon grace, we feel starved sometimes. And so we use blessings for our own benefit, thinking that serving ourselves will make the hunger of our hearts go away. The blessing of money is traded for possessions that clutter our days and tire our minds. The blessing of natural resources is transformed into lavishly appointed rooms that are hardly used. The blessing of physical intimacy is squandered on all kinds of sexual jazz that drones on in one monotonous key. We graze and graze on blessings and acquire a taste for cud. It seems like we'd learn that the blessing binge wouldn't make us happy and that only the Holy Spirit can teach us what we need to know and how we need to live.

I use the word *need* here carefully. We don't need to do anything to earn blessings or make God love us. Jesus took care of that. But if we want to find a measure of peace and fulfillment in this life, if we want to minimize the frustrating journey from orgy to vomitorium, we need to recognize that God's gifts—of healing or anything else—are best celebrated with God and shared with others in the name of God. In other words, the best thing to do with a divine gift is to give it to somebody else. The best use of a body made whole is that it be an instrument of comfort to others. The best use of a big bank account is to share its contents with those who have nothing. The best use of strong arms is to pick up somebody who has fallen.

Obviously, service is faithful. That's beyond debate. What's not so obvious is that loving service in the name of Jesus Christ is that mysterious blessing we've all been looking for. Blessings wilt when hoarded. When shared, they blossom, and so do we. The gifts we receive end up being burdens when they aren't realized by our passing them on.

And so what's the blessing—the fact that I can put a sentence together, or that you and I are together in this moment, both of us looking at Christ, who has sent the gift of all gifts—the Holy Spirit—to bind us together in peace, compassion, and understanding? The gift is passing on the gift.

That's why Simon's mother-in-law served Jesus and the others. The miracle wasn't only that Jesus healed her but that she realized her blessing by doing something pretty simple: bringing them some food and making them comfortable.

Invitation to Reflection ✿

✿ Simon's mother-in-law responded to her healing with service. How might her example offer us a positive model of discipleship? How would it be possible to turn her story into a model for workaholism and ill health? In the end, what does the unexpected teaching in this story of healing say to our society's understanding of rights and responsibilities?

✿ Take a moment to reflect on the relationship between the life of faith and rights and responsibilities. What sorts of things do you take to be God-given rights? What are our responsibilities in the eyes of God?

A SACRED TENSION

John 7:10–24

¹⁰But after his brothers had gone to the festival, then he also went, not publicly but as it were in secret. ¹¹The Jews were looking for him at the festival and saying, "Where is he?" ¹²And there was considerable complaining about him among the crowds. While some were saying, "He is a good man," others were saying, "No, he is deceiving the crowd." ¹³Yet no one would speak openly about him for fear of the Jews.

¹⁴About the middle of the festival Jesus went up into the temple and began to teach. ¹⁵The Jews were astonished at it, saying, "How does this man have such learning, when he has never been taught?" ¹⁶Then Jesus answered them, "My teaching is not mine but his who sent me. ¹⁷Anyone who resolves to do the will of God will know whether the teaching is from God or whether I am speaking on my own. ¹⁸Those who speak on their own seek their own glory; but the one who seeks the glory of him who sent him is true, and there is nothing false in him.

19"Did not Moses give you the law? Yet none of you keeps the law. Why are you looking for an opportunity to kill me?" 20The crowd answered, "You have a demon! Who is trying to kill you?" 21Jesus answered them, "I performed one work, and all of you are astonished. 22Moses gave you circumcision (it is, of course, not from Moses, but from the patriarchs), and you circumcise a man on the sabbath. 23If a man receives circumcision on the sabbath in order that the law of Moses may not be broken, are you angry with me because I healed a man's whole body on the sabbath? 24Do not judge by appearances, but judge with right judgment."

❦ ❦ ❦

THE UNEXPECTED TEACHING:
Even Jesus humbled himself to the wisdom and will of God the Father.

John 7:10–24 includes a layering of ideas, all of which deserve attention; however, the idea that speaks to the United States today is in this verse: "Those who speak on their own seek their own glory." Over the years, I've reflected a lot on how Jesus spoke and for what purpose. Slowly, I've come to develop an interior alarm system when listening to myself or others speak. At certain moments, the bell goes off, and I ask, Why am I speaking (or why is another person speaking)? Is it to provide genuine insight into the situation or topic of discussion? Is it to provide appropriate direction, comfort, or challenge? Does it promote wholeness or health in some way? Will the words lead to intimacy? Or am I speaking to make myself look smart, pious, or clever? In short, am I flapping my tongue to cooperate in some fashion with the reign of God, or am I seeking to glorify myself?

Asking these questions in a way that doesn't turn us away from the grace of God or shove us chin-first into a narcissistic pool is tricky. The first thing that needs to be said is that no matter how dazzling or dim our words may be, God embraces us as we are. Any beauty or brains we've got comes directly from the reality of God's love for us, but we can't seem to trust that fact. And so lots of us—myself included—dress ourselves with fabrics and sentences designed to glorify ourselves. Vanity's got a good grip on most of us. Just try walking by a storefront window without checking yourself out.

Vanity wouldn't be so bad if it stopped with worrying about whether we look fat or our hair is sticking up, but such concerns are just hors d'oeuvres before the main course of self-interest and glorification. Much of what we do benefits nobody but ourselves and sometimes actually hurts others. If we take an indecently large salary ourselves, for example, and pay our employees a wage that keeps them one week ahead of homelessness, we benefit from another's hardship. If we call our spouse or children stupid, we may feel superior, but we do so at their expense. Now, let's stop for a qualifier. I don't intend to preach false humility, self-mortification, or a sackcloth-and-ashes piety. I do want to suggest instead a measure of self-awareness adequate to ensure that we are living with a simple dignity that God would smile upon but not so much that we neurotically monitor ourselves into constant, joy-stealing inspection of every joke, ice cream cone, or pair of socks. This is an ideal, of course, a next-to-impossible sacred tension, but such a degree of self-knowledge is a faithfully ambitious goal in the context of God's gift of human freedom.

The question is, How can we attempt to live as cocreators of God's reign by speaking and acting on behalf of that reign and not for our own sake? How can we know, in a given situation, whether we're seeking our own glory or the glory of the One who sends us? When a conversation turns mean-spirited, for whom do we speak? When our salary is on the table, for whom do we negotiate? When we're buying and furnishing a house, on whose behalf do we sign loan papers? When we pick out a car, is vanity or transportation being served?

These questions suggest two realities. First, such reflection, when carried too far, can strip sweetness and spontaneity from life. I don't think God calls us to live with brows forever furrowed and backs bent under the weight of every decision. We are human beings: our frailties come spilling out of us minute by minute; were this not so, we would have no use for God's grace. Only by finding joy and power within this grace can we engage in self-reflection without wilting into despair. Second, we are called to the process of discernment, for there is no such product as the perfect human, beyond Jesus of Nazareth. It's easy to buy into the notion that if we but try hard enough, we can eventually attain a life lived wholly for the sake of God. This won't happen, but at least we can wake up each day asking God to give us the awareness to speak and act in accord with God's will.

We hope to live, then, in holy awareness. When in the Holy Spirit we do so, we begin to awaken from what liberation theologian Jon Sobrino calls "the sleep of inhumanity," and we can see some of the ways in which our words and deeds not only serve ourselves but tarnish and mar the will of God.

This discernment process is messy. We never quite know whether we act for God, for ourselves, or (blessing of blessings!) for both. In a prayer from *Thoughts in Solitude,* Thomas Merton includes words that might speak for all of us as we try to "seek the glory of the God who sends us": "the fact that I think that I am following your will does not mean that I am actually doing so. But I believe that the desire to please you does in fact please you. And I hope I have that desire in all that I am doing. I hope that I will never do anything apart from that desire. And I know that if I do this you will lead me by the right road though I may know nothing about it. Therefore will I trust you always." Amen.

Invitation to Reflection

- Cultivating an awareness of why we do what we do is a part of discerning what a life centered in Jesus Christ looks like day by day. Where are you in your journey of faith these days? Do you feel a calling to center your life in Jesus Christ?

- Recall a conversation you've had in the past few days. Can you think of things that you said that tore another person down for no good reason? Why do you suppose you engaged in such talk? What need of yours—positive or negative—did the words satisfy? This kind of reflection can be unsettling. Remember, the goal here is to cultivate awareness, not beat ourselves up. We "all have sinned and fall short of the glory of God" (Romans 3:23).
- One way to give glory to God is by sharing our faith stories. Our stories give glory to God not only when they're joyful and moving but also when they include doubt and disbelief. What's the story of your relationship with God? What's the story of your relationship with the church? What are your moments of joy and struggle?

THE CLASSROOM ON THE ROAD

John 14:18–31

18"I will not leave you orphaned; I am coming to you. 19In a little while the world will no longer see me, but you will see me; because I live, you also will live. 20On that day you will know that I am in my Father, and you in me, and I in you. 21They who have my commandments and keep them are those who love me; and those who love me will be loved by my Father, and I will love them and reveal myself to them." 22Judas (not Iscariot) said to him, "Lord, how is it that you will reveal yourself to us, and not to the world?" 23Jesus answered him, "Those who love me will keep my word, and my Father will love them, and we will come to them and make our home with them. 24Whoever does not love me does not keep my words; and the word that you hear is not mine, but is from the Father who sent me.

^{25} "I have said these things to you while I am still with you. ^{26} But the Advocate, the Holy Spirit, whom the Father will send in my name, will teach you everything, and remind you of all that I have said to you. ^{27} Peace I leave with you; my peace I give to you. I do not give to you as the world gives. Do not let your hearts be troubled, and do not let them be afraid. ^{28} You heard me say to you, 'I am going away, and I am coming to you.' If you loved me you would rejoice that I am going to the Father, because the Father is greater than I. ^{29} And now I have told you this before it occurs, so that when it does occur, you may believe. ^{30} I will no longer talk much with you, for the ruler of this world is coming. He has no power over me; ^{31} but I do as the Father has commanded me, so that the world may know that I love the Father. Rise, let us be on our way."

✄ ✄ ✄

THE UNEXPECTED TEACHING:
Jesus' disciples learned along the way.

My favorite passage in all of Scripture is John 14:1–17:26, a collection of chapters commonly referred to as Jesus' Farewell Discourse to his disciples. Nowhere else in the Bible is there more love and concern expressed as when Jesus tried to comfort and instruct his disciples in the hours before his arrest, torture, and crucifixion. They had given up everything to follow him, and now he had to die. Jesus knew they would face fear and grief, so he found different ways to help them conceptualize hope in the midst of great loss. He told them of dwelling places he would prepare for them, of his coming for them again in the future, and of the Holy Spirit, who would come to teach them.

In the middle of such a moving, significant collection of verses, "Rise, let us be on our way" seems incongruous. One moment, Jesus was leaving peace with the Twelve, then he said, "Let's go," then he picked right up again with "I am the true vine, and my Father is the vinegrower" (15:1). Maybe "Rise, let us be on our way" is just an awkward attempt at transition on the part of this Gospel writer. Or maybe the reference to "our way" is neat literary echoing of "the way." In writing this meditation, I might be accused of thinking too much about seven little words in the middle of a discourse that has many more important ideas to flesh out. Still, the implication of Jesus' statement is striking: at least part of his good-bye to his disciples took place on the road. We aren't told whether the gang stopped somewhere to rest and talk some more, but they probably did, as John 18 begins with, "After Jesus had spoken these words, he went out with his disciples across the Kidron valley to a place where there was a garden, which he and his disciples entered."

Even as the disciples were literally moving along on their journey toward Jesus' crucifixion, they were also learning about what that event would mean for them and for the world. There was no way for them to stop time until they got the whole disturbing, confusing business figured out. They had to walk and talk at the same time. Their instruction and reflection took place in the midst of the very event about which they were learning. The rising and being on their way took place not after they'd learned but as they learned—and as they began to process their emotional response to what was happening. In fact, a major part of what they learned was in the very act of hitting the trail.

The disciples were involved in a learn-as-you-go model of teaching, which could get pretty sloppy. Of course, if we stop and think about it, this is the way education works. We can gain skill in doing things only as we do them. If we, or the disciples, wait around for complete, flawless knowledge before we act, we're not going to get very far. Because learning is a process, we have to accept that lots of mistakes get made. Fortunately, as any experienced teacher will say, goof-ups provide wonderfully helpful teaching moments. The downside to the process of learning is that mistakes do occur. If a teenager mows the grass in a stupid way, no terrible harm is done, but if a brain surgeon says, "Oops," we've got trouble.

As Christians, we often feel like ill-prepared brain surgeons when we are faced with the challenges of discipleship. We're afraid of making the wrong decision (for example, saying the wrong thing to a friend struggling with depression or giving money to a homeless person who might use it to buy booze). We're reluctant to reach out because we don't want to mess up or engage in an effort that's ineffective. Heaven forbid we should waste our resources! That would be poor stewardship.

Sometimes, I hear Jesus say to us, "Rise, let us be on our way," and I hear myself and others respond, "Let's not. How about we stay here until we're sure about what to do or say?" Nevertheless, in the middle of our learning and growing, Jesus says, "Let's go. There's ministry to do."

"But I don't know how to do ministry," we say. Or "But I don't know if I can handle where it is you want me to go. It might hurt too much. Can't I just stay here until you're all done teaching me?"

"The classroom is on the road," Jesus says, "You'll learn to love by touching the unloved. You'll learn to handle hurt by walking into hurt. You'll learn to be a disciple by walking with me, even when you feel afraid and ill prepared. You'll learn to bear fruit by bearing fruit. Rise. Follow me."

Invitation to Reflection 🦋

- My old college theater teacher used to say, "Comedy is pain." We might also say, "Learning is pain" because some of our most powerful lessons come through our mistakes. What significant lessons have you learned through suffering or mistakes? Has what you've learned been worth the pain?

- Have you avoided doing things because you were afraid of goofing up? What are some examples? Reflect for a moment on the fear associated with making mistakes. What exactly is it we're afraid of?

- When is it healthy to make sure we have all our ducks in a row before we act? What kinds of situations call for caution and careful planning? (If your answer to these last questions involves money, devote some extra time to this issue. Is there anything special about money? Does money hold a special place for us? Does it deserve this place?)

EXTRAVAGANT LOVE

John 12:1–8

¹Six days before the Passover Jesus came to Bethany, the home of Lazarus, whom he had raised from the dead. ²There they gave a dinner for him. Martha served, and Lazarus was one of those at the table with him. ³Mary took a pound of costly perfume made of pure nard, anointed Jesus' feet, and wiped them with her hair. The house was filled with the fragrance of the perfume. ⁴But Judas Iscariot, one of his disciples (the one who was about to betray him), said, ⁵"Why was this perfume not sold for three hundred denarii and the money given to the poor?" ⁶(He said this not because he cared about the poor, but because he was a thief; he kept the common purse and used to steal what was put into it.) ⁷Jesus said, "Leave her alone. She bought it so that she might keep it for the day of my burial. ⁸You always have the poor with you, but you do not always have me."

❧ ❧ ❧

THE UNEXPECTED TEACHING:

The One with nowhere to lay his head permitted an extravagant moment.

There are a couple of tempting details tucked into the crevices of John 12. It is interesting to note that just after this passage, the Gospel tells us that the chief priests planned to kill Lazarus as well as Jesus because people believed in Jesus because of him. Those chief priests were nasty. Also notable is the remark that Judas was swiping funds from the community purse. We think that church groups ought to be able to work together peacefully and avoid trouble, but Jesus' own council had an embezzler, among other things.

The most remarkable aspect of this passage is that Jesus did, in fact, allow Mary to anoint him with the costly perfume. The heavy of the story, Judas, got to be the killjoy, observing that the perfume could be sold for three hundred denarii, which the *New Oxford Annotated Bible* says was equivalent to a laborer's yearly salary. I could see myself saying exactly the same thing Judas did, mainly because, although I haven't taken a formal vow of poverty, I do think that life lived simply is faithful to the gospel as I understand it. Pouring what today would be (what shall we say?) $25,000 worth of sweet-smelling gunk over anybody's feet seems foolishly extravagant, especially when one person dies of a simple hunger-related condition every two and a half seconds. Most days, I find myself with Judas, at least in this one sentiment.

But Jesus has something to teach us. There are moments when extravagance is called for. The question is, What do such moments look like? Fortunately, Jesus was involved with other extravagant moments; maybe by looking at them we can understand why Mary was right and Judas was wrong.

The first example I can think of is not a single Bible passage but the whole Gospel of Luke, in which there are seventeen references to Jesus eating with outcasts and sinners. It seems that Jesus' way of connecting to folks was by sitting at the table with them. But it wasn't just that Jesus ate and drank a lot in Luke but that he did so as a matter of habit with the castoffs of society and in a social situation that was particularly sensitive in his day. As R. Alan Culpepper writes, "Pharisees maintained a separation from others and ate only with those who, like them, observed the laws of purity." Jesus would have been expected to do the same, so his excess is, well, doubly excessive. Not only was he eating all the time in Luke, but he was also doing it with the wrong people.

Jesus' triumphal entry into Jerusalem, which we observe on Palm Sunday, was another excessive moment. Folks making a carpet of palms for Jesus as he made his way down the road on a donkey's colt and shouting, "Hosanna! Blessed is the one who comes in the name of the Lord—the King of Israel!" (John 12:13) certainly constituted a lavish amount of attention for Jesus.

The most excessive moment I know of in all of Scripture, however, is the crucifixion. Think of his death. He was publicly humiliated, whipped until the flesh was hanging from his body, and nailed to a cross to bleed to death and suffocate. Lots of other deaths would have been a lot less extravagant, and let's not forget that Jesus could have escaped that fate had he wished to do so. All he had to do was say the right things to the religious leaders, or, as he said himself, call upon the angels for assistance (Matthew 25:41), and he would have been off the hook.

What all of these moments of extravagance have in common is love. Either people were loving and worshiping Jesus or he was loving them. In each case, an overflowing of love brought about the moment of excess. When Jesus ate and drank with tax collectors and sinners and outcasts, he did so out of love for them. It was for them that he came. When Jesus was on the road into Jerusalem, people loved him—in a fickle, human way, but loved him nevertheless. When Mary poured perfume over his feet and wiped them with her hair, she did so out of love. In fact, we might even speculate that Jesus was more concerned about giving Mary a way to release her love than he was about the nard itself. Not long before, Jesus had raised her brother, Lazarus, from the dead. One can't help but imagine the affection all in that family must have had for Jesus.

And when Jesus poured himself out for all people on the cross, he did so out of love. His whole life was motivated by his love for people, his desire to see their suffering ended, his longing that they accept his embrace. And his last act, allowing nails to be pounded into his hands and feet, was bitterly excessive, but it was also the result of Jesus' love for creation, that it might be right with God.

So extravagance had its day, but always in the context of love. It's worth mentioning that Jesus didn't come into Jerusalem behind a team of Clydesdales, that his meals with outcasts didn't take place in fancy restaurants, that Mary didn't have to remove Jesus' Bruno Magli shoes before anointing his feet with that perfume worth a shop worker's yearly take.

Extravagant acts grow out of extravagant love.

Invitation to Reflection

- ✒ What are some of your memories of people showing you love in unexpected and thoughtful ways?

- ✒ Faithful extravagance ought to be grounded in love. Can you think of cases in which extravagance was based on something other than love? In such cases, what was the giving really about? Were there any ways in which the giving did more harm than good?

- ✒ Have you ever been part of a situation in which either giving seemed to get out of hand or givers tried to outdo one another? What do you think such giving is ultimately about? Do you ever find yourself caught up in such situations? How do you feel about or deal with times of uncomfortable giving?

THE LORD'S PRAYER

Matthew 6:5–15

5 "And whenever you pray, do not be like the hypocrites; for they love to stand and pray in the synagogues and at the street corners, so that they may be seen by others. Truly I tell you, they have received their reward. 6 But whenever you pray, go into your room and shut the door and pray to your Father who is in secret; and your Father who sees in secret will reward you.

7 "When you are praying, do not heap up empty phrases as the Gentiles do; for they think that they will be heard because of their many words. 8 Do not be like them, for your Father knows what you need before you ask him. 9 Pray then in this way:

Our Father in heaven.

Hallowed be your name.

10 Your kingdom come.

Your will be done,

on earth as it is in heaven.

^{11}Give us this day our daily bread.

^{12}And forgive us our debts,

>   as we also have forgiven our debtors.

^{13}And do not bring us to the time of trial,

>   but rescue us from the evil one.

> *^{14}For if you forgive others their trespasses, your heavenly Father will also forgive you; ^{15}but if you do not forgive others, neither will your Father forgive your trespasses."*

⚹ ⚹ ⚹

THE UNEXPECTED TEACHING:
The Lord's Prayer was for the community.

As people shaped by Western culture, we tend to think about ourselves first and about others later, almost as an afterthought. If we give a donation to charity, we want to make sure that we have a record of the transaction so that we can get a tax break. If we buy a valuable antique for a few bucks at a yard sale, that's no problem. Let the buyer—and the seller—beware.

Even our spirituality tends to be individualistic. When we think about life after death, we hope we'll make it to heaven, and, by the way, it'd be great if everyone else does, too. When we think of sins, we think of our own, hope we can stop committing them, pray we can be forgiven them.

In nearly every way, our identity is wrapped up in our own selves, needs, worries, rights (most of the time), and responsibilities (once in a while). But this is not the only way of conceiving of ourselves and the world around us. The use of the first person plural (*we* and *our*) in the Lord's Prayer points to a sense of identity grounded in community, in this case, Israel. As people of the modern Western world, we have to work hard to connect with a sense of self that is grounded not in our own strengths and shortcomings but in the collective attributes of our communities.

One can't read the Old Testament without sensing that the people of God saw themselves as a group at least as much as autonomous individuals. Maybe more to the point, it's clear that God saw the people as a people, not as persons. I say this not presuming to know the mind of God but by observing that the Old Testament, by and large, is a story of God's faithfulness to God's people. True, individuals such as Abraham and Sarah are the foci of sacred episodes, and the stories of their relationship with Yahweh teach us about how we as separate persons might live; nevertheless, what happens to them is important because of what it means for Israel, the whole people of God. And the ebb and flow of their story in the Old Testament is God's faithfulness in spite of the people's repeated unfaithfulness.

When we pray the Lord's Prayer, we can't help but pray as individuals. It's just part of who we are. But the Lord's Prayer, as well as other parts of Christian liturgy, take on an authenticity and richness when we say or sing them as a community.

What does it mean, for example, to say, "Give us this day our daily bread" as a community? Obviously, it means something much larger than "Give me this day enough to eat." In his *Small Catechism*, Martin Luther writes that "daily bread" includes "everything our bodies need." When we say "us" not as "me" but as "all children of God and me, too," we're praying for nothing less than the sustenance of all people.

And when we say, "forgive us our debts as we also have forgiven our debtors," we pray not only about our individual debts but those of our entire community. My parish family, for example, may be slow in recognizing suffering in its neighborhood and even slower to respond. In the Lord's Prayer, we confess our corporate debts and recognize our responsibility to forgive those who have hurt the church.

Grounding ourselves in a communal identity not only deepens the Lord's Prayer but also the entire Christian liturgy. In many Lutheran churches, worship begins with the Brief Order for Confession and Forgiveness. Those assembled say, "Most merciful God, we confess that we are in bondage to sin and cannot free ourselves. We have sinned against you in thought, word, and deed, by what we have done, and by what we have left undone. We have not loved you with our whole heart; we have not loved our neighbors as ourselves. For the sake of your Son, Jesus Christ, have mercy on us. Forgive us, renew us, and lead us, so that we may delight in your will and walk in your ways, to the glory of your holy name. Amen." When I read this and understood "we" to mean "the church," it was as if I was reading the confession for the first time. When I thought of bondage to sin, I didn't think about my own failures and condition of alienation from God but about the church's sinfulness in a sinful world. I thought about Martin Luther's terribly unfortunate polemic against Jews, the church's oppression of women, and its frequent reluctance to put its own safety aside and stand with the poor in ways that would leave no doubt as to what God we worship.

I make these observations not to cast stones. Like my church, I'm in bondage to sin and cannot free myself. In fact, one of the reasons I love the church is that I know it to be so much like me and all other people: fully human, unable to understand the forces that prevent it from doing what it ought to do and that compel it to do what it shouldn't do. Indeed, what Paul says of himself in his letter to the Romans (7:15), we can say of the church: "For I do not understand my own actions. For I do not do what I want, but I do the very thing I hate." As a member of my community of faith, I'm in denial when I pretend that the church is not really a human institution, not engaging on a corporate level in the same struggles I face as an individual.

Reading the Lord's Prayer and the rest of the Christian liturgy as part of the large "we" helps us to weather anger, disappointment, and chagrin when we see the church not behaving as we think it should. We don't behave as we should either. The church needs God's grace and mercy as much as each believer does. And when we remember this, we can love and embrace the church in its human weakness and celebrate the Spirit's working through it as an imperfect instrument of God's will.

Invitation to Reflection

- It's depressing to admit that we live in a broken world, but until we fully enter into and own our brokenness, we can't hope to grow from it, whether as individuals or communities. What are some of the sins of the church that you think we need to own up to and grow from? Can you think of sins we're reluctant to confess?

- With the help of the Holy Spirit, we manage to do some good in this world. Reflect upon times when your congregation or group of friends or coworkers did some good that could not have happened if you had been acting alone. In such cases, we might feel like the sum of our efforts is greater than the individual parts. Have you ever experienced this? What was it like?

- Read the Lord's Prayer again. What line or image speaks to you the most right now? Explain why.

HEALING SHAME

Mark 5:21–43

²¹ *When Jesus had crossed again in the boat to the other side, a great crowd gathered around him; and he was by the sea.* ²² *Then one of the leaders of the synagogue named Jairus came and, when he saw him, fell at his feet* ²³ *and begged him repeatedly, "My little daughter is at the point of death. Come and lay your hands on her, so that she may be made well, and live."* ²⁴ *So he went with him.*

And a large crowd followed him and pressed in on him. ²⁵ *Now there was a woman who had been suffering from hemorrhages for twelve years.* ²⁶ *She had endured much under many physicians, and had spent all that she had; and she was no better, but rather grew worse.* ²⁷ *She had heard about Jesus, and came up behind him in the crowd and touched his cloak,* ²⁸ *for she said, "If I but touch his clothes, I will be made well."* ²⁹ *Immediately her hemorrhage stopped; and she felt in her body that she was healed of her disease.* ³⁰ *Immediately aware that power had gone forth from him, Jesus turned about in the crowd and said, "Who touched my clothes?" 31 And his disciples said to him, "You see the crowd pressing in on you; how can you say, 'Who touched me?'" 32 He looked all around to see who had done it. 33 But the woman, knowing what had happened to her, came in fear and trembling, fell down before him, and told him the whole truth. 34 He said to her, "Daughter, your faith has made you well; go in peace, and be healed of your disease."*

35 While he was still speaking, some people came from the leader's house to say, "Your daughter is dead. Why trouble the teacher any further?" 36 But overhearing what they said, Jesus said to the leader of the synagogue, "Do not fear, only believe." 37 He allowed no one to follow him except Peter, James, and John, the brother of James. 38 When they came to the house of the leader of the synagogue, he saw a commotion, people weeping and wailing loudly. 39 When he had entered, he said to them, "Why do you make a commotion and weep? The child is not dead but sleeping." 40 And they laughed at him. Then he put them all outside, and took the child's father and mother and those who were with him, and went in where the child was. 41 He took her by the hand and said to her, "Talitha cum," which means, "Little girl, get up!" 42 And immediately the girl got up and began to walk about (she was twelve years of age). At this they were overcome with amazement. 43 He strictly ordered them that no one should know this, and told them to give her something to eat.

✶ ✶ ✶

THE UNEXPECTED TEACHING:

Jesus brought the hemorrhaging woman back into the community.

Sometimes our knowledge of Jesus' culture doesn't have all that great an impact on our reading of the Gospels, but in the case of this scriptural passage, if we don't understand the world of the story, we miss the bulk of its teaching. There are actually two stories, one tucked inside another. The story of the hemorrhaging woman takes place in the middle of Jesus' journey to raise Jairus's daughter from the dead. Much is made of Mark's weaving these accounts one into the other—and rightfully so.

For me, however, the unexpected teaching involves the woman who touched Jesus' cloak after having apparently fought her way through the crowd to get to him. On the surface, the woman's actions speak of her faith and of Jesus' healing presence. All she had to do was touch his clothes, and she would be made well. So, we think, Jesus was just dripping with healing power. It encircled him like perfume; that's how holy he was.

Central to her healing, however, was a detail many of us miss. The woman had severe menstrual bleeding. I expect most readers know this. What may not be so well known is that her condition made her an outcast in society, like a leper. Actually, her situation was worse than that of an outcast, if that is possible. To her community, this woman was fundamentally unclean. Her condition, obviously a central reality in her life, reduced her to a smudge on holiness. Touching her, or being touched by her, rendered one impure. The Old Testament book of Leviticus, which expresses the norms that guided Jesus' culture, goes on at length about what was impure and how to get impure things pure again. Leviticus 15:25–30 describes how a hemorrhaging woman would have been regarded by those around her:

> If a woman has a discharge of blood for many days, not at the time of her impurity, or if she has a discharge beyond the time of her impurity, all the days of the discharge she shall continue in uncleanness; as in the days of her impurity, she shall be unclean. Every bed on which she lies during all the days of her discharge shall be treated as the bed of her impurity; and everything on which she sits shall be unclean, as in the uncleanness of her impurity. Whoever touches these things shall be unclean, and shall wash his clothes, and bathe in water, and be unclean until the evening. If she is cleansed of her discharge, she shall count seven days, and after that she shall be clean. On the eighth day she shall take two turtledoves or two pigeons and bring them to the priest at the entrance of the tent of meeting. The priest shall offer one for a sin offering and the other for a burnt offering; and the priest shall make atonement on her behalf before the Lord for her unclean discharge.

So what does it mean that the hemorrhaging woman touched Jesus? After all, a lot of desperate people touched or wanted to touch Jesus, and the Gospels are full of people whose faith made them well. Her action is important, but the fact is, others did the same thing. What stands out in this account is how Jesus responded to her touch. The woman knew that Jesus might be angry because she was unclean. Wittingly or not, she rendered Jesus ritually impure; what's more, in a way she stole healing from him. So he had a couple of potential reasons to be upset with her.

It's significant that he listened and had compassion for her. I can only imagine the story she must have told: twelve years of suffering and shame, twelve years of investing hope in one physician after another and being disappointed. How tired, powerless, and desperate she must have been—not to mention anemic! Jesus' listening penetrated the social discomfort of her relentless menstrual bleeding and heard what she was going through as a whole person.

Lest we think we've gotten past the old-fashioned taboos of Jesus' day, it's worth reckoning our own social discomfort for a minute. We're still squeamish about women's menstrual periods. At age eleven, my daughter Elena senses that this matter is to be discussed quietly, discreetly. A few months ago Kathy, my wife, and I went with her to buy *The Period Book* so that she could read up on periods, puberty, and guys. When we got home, she called a neighbor girl, and together they went into Elena's bedroom and read the book to each other in whispers. The whole enterprise was sweet and healthy. Although the girls were whispering about "woman stuff," they were talking, and they knew that Kathy and I knew that they were talking and imagining and giggling and reassuring each other.

Nice as Elena's huddled talk was, there was some shame mixed in too. And if this is how she felt, the shame of the hemorrhaging woman must have been layer upon layer. In his compassion, Jesus did a lot more than heal her from menstrual bleeding. First, he called her "daughter" and wished her peace. Not only was he not angry that she touched him, but her ritual impurity didn't even appear to enter the equation. If a modern reader of the Bible was wondering whether Jesus was sensitive to the concerns of women, he or she could do worse than to consult the story of the hemorrhaging woman. Jesus' exchange with the Samaritan woman at the well (John 4:1–43) and his relationship with Mary Magdalene also speak to his communion with and acceptance of women. Second, Jesus not only addressed the woman's physical ailment but he also opened the door for her reentry into the community. It's curious that Jesus' last words to the woman were "be healed of your disease," for here he stated what has already been accomplished. Maybe the disease he referenced at this point was the woman's loneliness and shame.

To us, Jesus' healing of a nameless, bleeding woman seems almost commonplace. In fact, in being touched by her and responding with understanding and compassion, Jesus raised love above all other concerns. He continued down the road to Jairus's house in what the law would have said was an impure state, and he entered the synagogue leader's house, taking Jairus and his wife to their daughter's bedside. (Did he take them by the hand?) Then, he took their daughter's hand and gave her life again. By this time, Jesus had gotten the nameless woman's (sacred) impurity all over everything: Jairus, his wife, their house, their daughter, Lord knows who and what else. And miraculously, despite that woman's twelve years of bleeding and impurity, the dead lived again.

Invitation to Reflection ❧

- ✴ Had Jesus been wrapped up in just getting to Jairus's house, he might not have noticed the woman's touch at all. With a minor detour, he changed a life. Have you ever experienced something tremendously important and unexpected on your way to some other place? What have you learned from pauses or detours on your journey? Are you open to interruptions in your routine? Is the Holy Spirit sometimes tapping you on the shoulder?

- ✴ It does us good to remember that Jesus didn't shy away from things that make folks squeamish. Where do you think you or your community of faith are being called into the world's points of awkwardness and discomfort? We can be pretty sure that where people are reluctant to talk about difficult matters, the love of Jesus is desperately needed.

✎ There are "hemorrhaging" people all around us, people whom the world regards as smudges. Who are they? Reflect upon Jesus' call to bring them into community. How might we do so?

The PERILOUS

TEACHINGS

"Accordingly, though Jesus loved Martha and her sister and Lazarus, after having heard that Lazarus was ill, he stayed two days longer in the place where he was." (JOHN 11:5–6)

IGNORING THE PREREQUISITE

John 2:1–11

¹On the third day there was a wedding in Cana of Galilee, and the mother of Jesus was there. ²Jesus and his disciples had also been invited to the wedding. ³When the wine gave out, the mother of Jesus said to him, "They have no wine." ⁴And Jesus said to her, "Woman, what concern is that to you and me? My hour has not yet come." ⁵His mother said to the servants, "Do whatever he tells you." ⁶Now standing there were six stone water jars for the Jewish rites of purification, each holding twenty or thirty gallons. ⁷Jesus said to them, "Fill the jars with water." And they filled them up to the brim. ⁸He said to them, "Now draw some out, and take it to the chief steward." So they took it. ⁹When the steward tasted the water that had become wine, and did not know where it came from (though the servants who had drawn the water knew), the steward called the bridegroom ¹⁰and said to him, "Everyone serves the good wine first, and then the inferior wine after the guests have become drunk. But you have kept the good wine until now." [11]*Jesus did this, the first of his signs, in Cana of Galilee, and revealed his glory; and his disciples believed in him.*

❡ ❡ ❡

THE UNEXPECTED TEACHING:
*The wedding feast had to run out of wine
for Jesus to perform a miracle.*

Just like Jesus' followers, we love signs and wonders. Any evidence of divine intervention in this world is delicious. It warms and braces our souls like a first swallow of cognac and, unfortunately, distracts us from real refreshment. Miracles, like alcohol, feel wet and wonderful going down, but a preoccupation with them leads to spiritual dehydration.

Our love of dazzling, immediate solutions leads us to focus on the miracle of Jesus transforming water into wine while ignoring the prerequisite for this beloved story: the party had to run out of wine before a miracle was possible. If everything went wonderfully, then Jesus didn't have a shot at "the first of his signs." There is an insult to Jesus implicit in our skipping over this fact. We want miracles without the crises that make them attractive in the first place.

The problem here isn't that we find wonders wonderful but that we are often surprised when we encounter the muck of life: illness, loss, failure, hardship, and so on. It would be stupid to deny that negative emotions are natural when painful events take place. If a marriage falls apart, the partners are probably going to feel a sense of failure. If a loved one dies, those left behind mourn. Even so, many folks unwittingly operate under the assumption that challenges aren't part of the ebb and flow of human existence. When things don't go our way, we feel somehow betrayed—by God, by others, or maybe just by life itself. If it weren't for bad luck, the saying goes, I wouldn't have any luck at all. The fact that this adage gets tossed around demonstrates that bad luck is common, to be expected.

My reason for pointing out the normalcy of muck is pretty simple. The wine is constantly running out. There's always some crisis to deal with, and we're ever in need of a miracle. One look at the experience of Jesus ought to tell us this. The authorities were a daily threat to him. Sometimes people in the crowds he taught wanted to throw him off a cliff. And of course, he was crucified. If that's not an emergency, I don't know what is.

To a child of God trying to find "the peace that passes all understanding" (Philippians 4:7), taking stock of just how tough Jesus' life was might be helpful. If we look at the accounts of our Lord's ministry and live our lives constantly blindsided and miffed by the many things that go wrong for us, we're neglecting a central teaching of the Gospels. Everybody who came to Jesus was desperate. He was the court of last appeal. Each miracle was preceded by days, sometimes years, of suffering and doubt. And in the case of Jesus' own crisis, the miracle came only after all seemed lost.

To live as disciples with intellectual integrity, we have to normalize challenge for ourselves. From the day we are born until the day we die, we endure our share of struggles. They never stop coming. What's more, today, as in Jesus' day, some folks experience the miraculous, but some don't. Nobody knows why. One thing is sure, however: if you don't have muck in the first place, you can't witness a miracle.

Invitation to Reflection

- At what point in your life have the greatest challenges come? How have you coped with them?

- Have you ever found yourself praying for a miracle? If so, what was going on at that time? What was the outcome of the situation, and what did you learn from the experience? How was your faith strengthened or challenged?

- In her book *The Presence of Absence,* Doris Grumbach tells of an encounter with God that was miraculous for her: "I was filled with a unique feeling of peace, an impression so intense that it seemed to expand into ineffable joy, a huge delight." Have you ever had such a miraculous meeting with God? If not, do you feel slighted? What's your story of God's presence in your life?

THE WEB OF
DISCERNMENT

Mark 3:1–6

¹ Again he entered the synagogue, and a man was there who had a withered hand. ²They watched him to see whether he would cure him on the sabbath, so that they might accuse him. ³And he said to the man who had the withered hand, "Come forward." ⁴Then he said to them, "Is it lawful to do good or to do harm on the sabbath, to save life or to kill?" But they were silent. ⁵He looked around at them with anger; he was grieved at their hardness of heart and said to the man, "Stretch out your hand." He stretched it out, and his hand was restored. ⁶The Pharisees went out and immediately conspired with the Herodians against him, how to destroy him.

❦ ❦ ❦

THE UNEXPECTED TEACHING:

Jesus' ministry caused trouble for both himself and his followers.

Liberation theologian Jon Sobrino writes, "We must realize that mercy that becomes justice will automatically be persecuted by the powerful, and therefore mercy must be clung to vigorously and consistently." The story of Jesus healing the man with the withered hand is one of dozens in which Jesus upset the powerful. The fact is, somebody was always mad at Jesus, who heard this world's cry for mercy and justice and responded.

To follow Jesus—closely now, not at a safe distance—means that people will be angry with us. This much is inevitable, if we get the gospel right at least some of the time. In parts of the world, as you read these words, people are being tortured because they follow Jesus. This very day, disciples will die as a direct result of heeding the call of Jesus to be merciful and just.

As the Pharisees saw it, Jesus was a threat to the fabric of their society. They didn't want him destroyed because he healed somebody but because he violated a system of rules that they depended on to hold their world together. As Jesus saw it, the man with the withered hand was being strangled in societal fabric. And so what was more important: to obey the rules or to cut free the person who was suffering? I can see myself in this situation and imagine my response. "Well," I'd probably say, "maybe I should enter into dialogue with the Pharisees and try to revise the observance of Sabbath so that folks could get healed. Just think," I'd go on, "if the observance of Sabbath could be changed, then many could be healed. This one guy will just have to wait so that more suffering people can be legally, safely healed in the future. After all, a withered hand is not life threatening, only an inconvenience." Before I knew it, I'd have the whole matter rationalized. I'd be off the hook, and the man's hand would still be withered. I'd be safe; the man would not. The Pharisees would be happy; the man would not.

The more I reflect on Jesus' behavior (and the older I get), the more I realize just how radical the gospel is. In the mirror it holds up to me, I see myself, stubborn and frightened. I don't want to get into trouble. I don't want people to be upset with me; I need to be loved and accepted. If people don't think well of me, my ego will be bruised.

Answering Jesus' call to mercy and justice and being a frail human being is a tough combination. In his *Address to the Christian Nobility of the German Nation,* Martin Luther called us to be "little Christs" to one another, and he knew what this could mean. For him, it meant hiding out in castles away from his home because religious authorities sought to have him killed. For most of us involved in the dialogue of this book, it might mean getting disowned by a loved one or being scolded at a church meeting.

This isn't a call to action; I haven't the right to issue one. I'm quite safe sitting in my study writing away, and as far as I know, no set of crosshairs is on me. Instead, this is simply a reminder. We ought not be surprised that people get mad at the gospel and at us when we manage to be faithful to it. The good news is not easy news. When we are merciful and just to those who suffer, we make a big mess for those who are comfortable. We love the "haves"—ourselves included—no less for their rage, but in the moments when we are most led by the Holy Spirit, we do not let that love turn to complacency. It is a reality that ending the suffering of some will probably create inconvenience for others.

So we find ourselves in a web of discernment. All that we do (or choose not to do) has a far-reaching, surprising impact. If, for example, I begin a ministry to folks with AIDS, do I make others in the church feel unsafe? If, like Dietrich Bonhoeffer, I collaborate in the plot to assassinate Hitler, do I alienate pacifists? The story of the man with the withered hand lets us know that, however we might decide to act, the follower of Jesus will certainly make people angry and threatened. Depend on it.

Invitation to Reflection ✨

✸ Individual Christians, and especially those of us who live out our faith in congregations, tend to place a high value on keeping the peace, on not rocking the boat, on not stirring the pot, and this may lead us to inaction. When conflict arises, we somehow feel as though we've blown it as Christians. How would you define taking a risk for the sake of the gospel? How would you describe yourself or your congregation in terms of taking risks for the sake of the gospel?

- Have people ever been angry with you because you've done something faithful? If so, how did you grow from the experience? Or how were you set back? What is your attitude now toward being faithful in the face of that reaction?

- What do you think of the idea that as Christians we're called to do things that upset people? Naturally, we don't want to go around getting people in a knot about nothing, but are there moments when being faithful compels us to be unpopular?

LAZARUS, GO IN!

John 11:1–44

1 Now a certain man was ill, Lazarus of Bethany, the village of Mary and her sister Martha. 2 Mary was the one who anointed the Lord with perfume and wiped his feet with her hair; her brother Lazarus was ill. 3 So the sisters sent a message to Jesus, "Lord, he whom you love is ill." 4 But when Jesus heard it, he said, "This illness does not lead to death; rather it is for God's glory, so that the Son of God may be glorified through it." 5 Accordingly, though Jesus loved Martha and her sister and Lazarus, 6 after having heard that Lazarus was ill, he stayed two days longer in the place where he was.

7 Then after this he said to the disciples, "Let us go to Judea again." 8 The disciples said to him, "Rabbi, the Jews were just now trying to stone you, and are you going there again?" 9 Jesus answered, "Are there not twelve hours of daylight? Those who walk during the day do not stumble, because they see the light of this world. 10 But those who walk at night stumble, because the light is not in them." 11 After saying this, he told them, "Our friend Lazarus has fallen asleep, but I am going there to awaken him." *12* The disciples said to him, "Lord, if he has fallen asleep, he will be all right." *13* Jesus, however, had been speaking about his death, but they thought that he was referring merely to sleep. *14* Then Jesus told them plainly, "Lazarus is dead. *15* For your sake I am glad I was not there, so that you may believe. But let us go to him." *16* Thomas, who was called the Twin, said to his fellow disciples, "Let us also go, that we may die with him."

17 When Jesus arrived, he found that Lazarus had already been in the tomb four days. *18* Now Bethany was near Jerusalem, some two miles away, *19* and many of the Jews had come to Martha and Mary to console them about their brother. *20* When Martha heard that Jesus was coming, she went and met him, while Mary stayed at home. *21* Martha said to Jesus, "Lord, if you had been here, my brother would not have died. *22* But even now I know that God will give you whatever you ask of him." *23* Jesus said to her, "Your brother will rise again." *24* Martha said to him, "I know that he will rise again in the resurrection on the last day." *25* Jesus said to her, "I am the resurrection and the life. Those who believe in me, even though they die, will live, *26* and everyone who lives and believes in me will never die. Do you believe this?" *27* She said to him, "Yes, Lord, I believe that you are the Messiah, the Son of God, the one coming into the world."

28 When she had said this, she went back and called her sister Mary, and told her privately, "The Teacher is here and is calling for you." *29* And when she heard it, she got up quickly and went to him. *30* Now Jesus had not yet come to the village, but was still at the place where Martha had met him. *31* The Jews who were with her in the house, consoling her, saw Mary get up quickly and go out. They followed her because they thought that she was going to the tomb to weep there. *32* When Mary came where Jesus was and saw him, she knelt at his feet and said to him, "Lord, if you had been here, my brother would not have died." *33* When Jesus saw her weeping, and the Jews who came with her also weeping, he was greatly disturbed in spirit and deeply moved. *34* He said, "Where have you laid him?" They said to him, "Lord, come and see." *35* Jesus began to weep. *36* So the Jews said, "See how he loved him!" *37* But some of them said, "Could not he who opened the eyes of the blind man have kept this man from dying?"

38 Then Jesus, again greatly disturbed, came to the tomb. It was a cave and a stone was lying against it. *39* Jesus said, "Take away the stone." Martha, the sister of the dead man, said to him, "Lord, already there is a stench because he has been dead four days." *40* Jesus said to her, "Did I not tell you that if you believed, you would see the glory of God?" *41* So they took away the stone. And Jesus looked upward and said, "Father, I thank you for having heard me. *42* I knew that you always hear me, but I have said this for the sake of the crowd standing here, so that they may believe that you sent me." *43* When he had said this, he cried with a loud voice, "Lazarus, come out!" *44* The dead man came out, his hands and feet bound with strips of cloth, and his face wrapped in a cloth. Jesus said to them, "Unbind him, and let him go."

✻ ✻ ✻

The Unexpected Teaching:

Lazarus had to go into his tomb.

We all have to enter the tomb someday—no choice in the matter. Until that day, however, we have lots of large and small tombs in our lives, places of fear and sorrow. One friend of mine was humiliated in the third grade during a math lesson when his teacher didn't believe he had to go to the bathroom. She soon found out he was telling the truth. That experience is a tomb for him. Another friend had boyfriends treat her like garbage when she was in high school. During dark moments, she still wonders whether she's worth much. That's a tomb.

And as if tombs like these aren't tough enough to live with, there are giant tombs, big, nasty, pitch-black, terrifying caves some folks have to live near all the time. Giant tombs: getting shot or watching someone else get shot; being the survivor of any kind of sexual abuse; walking away from home just after soldiers have burned it down and split up your family. I'm humbled by the strength it would take to live as a whole person in the midst of such tombs.

Conventional wisdom tells us to brick in the entrance to our tombs and move on! It's the stiff-upper-lip mentality. When I played Midget League baseball, the coach would always say to the kid who got hit in the shin, "Okay, kiddo, walk it off. Walk it off." Sometimes our pain comes from a wild pitch, and we're right to do the stoic thing and buck up. Lots of times, though, we try to walk off more serious wounds, and it just doesn't work.

In short, if we can't brick up a tomb, we've got to squeeze into it somehow and see what's in there. On a figurative level, this is what I think Jesus called Lazarus to do in this scriptural passage: "Get into that dark, stinking tomb and find out what's in there." And this is the unexpected teaching of Lazarus's story. He had to get dead before Jesus could resurrect him.

The same goes for us. If we don't walk all the way into our tombs, Jesus can't call us out. One big source of sorrow in my own life was watching somebody I loved die before managing to get all the way into her tombs. For years, she lived with one foot in and one foot out. She had a pretty good idea of what her issues were, but she never could bring herself to really work on them. I don't judge her for that. Tombs are scary. That being said, I think her fear of what was in her tombs ravaged her body, molested her mind, and, in the end, killed her. It is possible to die of truths ignored.

Obviously, the kind of work we're talking about (for example, counseling, reflection, revisiting old sorrows) is about as much fun as sliding down a twenty-foot razor blade. Still, Jesus allowed Lazarus to die. We might even say he called Lazarus into the tomb. We don't want to push this line of reasoning too far, however. It was not God's will for Lazarus, Mary, Martha, or anybody else to suffer, but given the realities of evil and human freedom, God called Lazarus and calls us as well to endure necessary suffering so we can participate in our own resurrection. By following God's call to enter our tombs, we are cocreators with God of our new selves, at least in the sense that we consent to God's work in us.

It's fitting that Lazarus came to life again in the very spot where he rotted and stank. When God gives us the courage to enter our tombs, we find life and renewal in the same space where we sat clenched up in a ball of suffering. That's the miracle, really. Death and birth bump into each other. The moment of our deepest despair is both sting of death and contraction of labor.

"Accordingly, though Jesus loved Martha and her sister and Lazarus, after having heard that Lazarus was ill, he stayed two days longer in the place where he was." Our tombs pepper the landscape, and Jesus doesn't just make them disappear. So we try to jump over them but fall on our chins. We try to go around them but end up running in circles. So Jesus waits for us to go inside them—two days, two years, two decades. Once inside, we discover ourselves, absolutely dependent on grace for every ounce of health and blessing. Then we can hear Jesus say, "Come out!"

Invitation to Reflection

ベ "You can't go home again." So goes the old saying. The problem is, sometimes we have to. Not only is home a place of nourishment and healing, but if we're going to be truthful, it's the site of some of our earliest and most long-lasting wounds. How do you think growing up in your household shaped you into the person you are today, warts and all?

✘ "You can't turn back the clock." So goes another old saying. But if you could climb into a time machine and change things about your past, what might you change? What things would you definitely want to keep the same?

✘ Can you think of struggles you've endured in your past that have made you a stronger, wiser person? What is it about some types of suffering that cause us to grow and mature—if only we can survive the process?

THE HOLY TENSION
OF GOD'S WILL

Mark 14:32–42

32 They went to a place called Gethsemane; and he said to his disciples, "Sit here while I pray." 33 He took with him Peter and James and John, and began to be distressed and agitated. 34 And he said to them, "I am deeply grieved, even to death; remain here, and keep awake." 35 And going a little farther, he threw himself on the ground and prayed that, if it were possible, the hour might pass from him. 36 He said, "Abba, Father, for you all things are possible; remove this cup from me; yet, not what I want, but what you want." 37 He came and found them sleeping; and he said to Peter, "Simon, are you asleep? Could you not keep awake one hour? 38 Keep awake and pray that you may not come into the time of trial; the spirit indeed is willing, but the flesh is weak." 39 And again he went away and prayed, saying the same words. 40 And once more he came and found them sleeping, for their eyes were very heavy; and they did not know

what to say to him. ⁴¹He came a third time and said to them,
"Are you still sleeping and taking your rest? Enough! The hour
has come; the Son of Man is betrayed into the hands of sinners.
⁴²Get up, let us be going. See, my betrayer is at hand."

⚹ ⚹ ⚹

The Unexpected Teaching:
Jesus suffered and prayed for the Father's will.

The picture of Jesus in Gethsemane gives us a
model for healthy spirituality. At first this might seem
an odd claim. We want our examples in the faith to be
at peace always, and Jesus in this account was anything
but peaceful. He got to thinking about what was going
to happen to him, went off by himself, threw himself on
the ground, and prayed that the crucifixion plan might
be aborted. He knew the type of death he'd endure, and
the picture wasn't appetizing. First, he'd go under a whip
designed specifically to tear the skin. Lots of people bled
to death from the whipping alone. Next, he'd carry his
instrument of execution to the appointed place and get
nailed to it, probably naked. In Luke's Gospel, as Jesus
prayed about his coming death, "his sweat became like
great drops of blood falling down on the ground"
(22:44).

Jesus understood how painful and humiliating his
death would be, and it scared him. His earnest prayer
was that, somehow, he wouldn't have to die so horribly.
In this moment, what Jesus said about Peter was also

true of himself: "the spirit indeed is willing, but the flesh is weak." For this reason, Jesus' prayer included two petitions: first, "remove this cup from me," and second, "not what I want, but what you want." The impulse of Jesus' earthly desires begged for a way out. Generally, human beings want to live. I remember a woman in the final stages of congestive heart failure who put the matter plainly. I asked her if she was at peace with dying. She looked at me as if I were as dumb as a turnip and said, "Well, nobody wants to die." I have to think there was a part of Jesus that didn't want to die. At the same time, he knew that what he was praying for might not be in harmony with God's will, so he placed his own wishes under the care of God's wishes.

This is the holy tension we learn from Jesus in Gethsemane: the voice of our own wills, often full of self-interest and self-promotion, has to be shaped by the acoustics of God's will, full of compassion for all that is. We can't pretend to understand or explain the mind of God, but Jesus teaches us that even in the face of what seems mostly costly and hurtful, we are to offer up our most fervent wishes in the context of the central petition of all prayers—that God's will be done.

There are more aggressive approaches to prayer that offer petitions almost as demands. The idea is that we are to be certain that our requests are compatible with God's will. My goal here isn't to establish the "right" theology of prayer but to acknowledge that there's more than one theology out there. But I'm always drawn to Jesus in Gethsemane. His experience there was quintessentially human. He was faced with circumstances he desperately wanted to avoid but sensed that he had to surrender himself to these circumstances for the sake of a purpose larger than his own.

Although this picture of Jesus' suffering is dark and troubling, its impression offers joyful applications. Often, I get absorbed by the power of my own wishes, but I find comfort in knowing that God does not. I've found that my most earnest prayers have been foolishness and that God's will for my life has proven infinitely preferable. I mention elsewhere in these meditations that many years ago I wanted nothing more than to be a poet. I now know that the poetry I cared to write was contrived to bring glory to me alone. It was a hollow enterprise. God has offered to me instead the challenge of giving my whole self to the divine will. Like Thomas Merton, I'm never quite sure whether what I want is what's best for me. And that's as it should be. Nearly everything I thought I wanted years ago I see today as rubbish. Honest! I also see that what Jesus wanted for himself in Gethsemane wasn't what was best for him or for the rest of humanity either.

Invitation to Reflection

✗ Some Christians are drawn to a theology of the cross, which is based on the belief that God in Jesus Christ is most present to us during moments of suffering. Have you experienced the presence of God during your most trying times? Sometimes, we can discern

God's presence only after the challenge has passed, only in prayerful hindsight. From this vantage point, can you see God's love and concern sustaining you?

ᛉ Perhaps you're going through a lousy stretch right now. Or maybe you can anticipate one coming soon. How does it feel to know that, just as God was present to Jesus in Gethsemane and on the cross, God is and will be present to you when your sweat becomes "like great drops of blood falling down on the ground"?

ᛉ What do you think about the prayer of Jesus in Gethsemane? How does Jesus' way of praying compare with yours? How do you talk with God?

GOSPEL GRAMMAR

Matthew 7:7–11

*7 "Ask, and it will be given you; search, and you will find;
knock, and the door will be opened for you. 8For everyone who
asks receives, and everyone who searches finds, and for everyone who knocks, the door will be opened. 9Is there anyone
among you who, if your child asks for bread, will give a stone?
10Or if the child asks for a fish, will give a snake? 11If you
then, who are evil, know how to give good gifts to your children, how much more will your Father in heaven give good
things to those who ask him!"*

❦ ❦ ❦

THE UNEXPECTED TEACHING:
*Jesus commanded his disciples to ask,
search, and knock.*

Grammar could bore a musk ox. When I used to
teach a college course called Remedial Writing (how's
that for a self-esteem-building name?), it was necessary

to talk about grammar. I hated it. The students would have rather watched tomatoes rot than talk about how language fits together. I suppose there are ways to make the study of syntax interesting, but I never figured out how.

A perverse residue left behind by my years of inflicting agony on students is an interest in how grammar works in the Bible, especially in Greek, the language in which the New Testament was originally written. What I've learned is that the grammar of Scripture matters. Pronouns refer to antecedents, and identifying the antecedent matters. Verbs are rendered in a certain tense, and the tense matters.

Greek verbs are rendered in particular tenses, persons, and moods, and the mood in this scriptural passage matters. Greek has the indicative, subjunctive, optative, infinitive, and imperative moods, as well as participles. I won't define all these, but the imperative mood is significant in this passage because it constitutes a command. In Greek, *ask, search,* and *knock* are presented in the imperative mood. They are commands, spoken as one might say, "Go snorkeling" or "Eat an avocado."

Ask, search, and *knock* could have been written in the subjunctive mood, which would have made the verbs conditional (that is, "if you ask, you will receive"). They could have been indicative verbs, simply stating a reality (as in "You search; you find" in the same way one might say, "You drive to the store; you buy bread"). But the three verbs in Matthew 7:7 are imperative. They're orders.

This grammatical quality tells us a lot. The first notion that gets blown out of the water is that questioning is bad. Some folks believe that in matters of religion, we're best off not thinking too much. Some carry this sensibility a step further and claim that questioning is actually dangerous, that to be inquisitive about issues central to Christianity is to flirt with blasphemy. As a result, lots of people stuff their thoughts deep down into their frightened psyches, and faith becomes an angst-ridden affair. Healthy, fruitful belief can never blossom because the soil has been secretly poisoned with denial. Certainly, there are moments when we all need to relax our clenched minds and simply accept things on faith, but honest doubt is preferable to dishonest faith. Matthew 7:7 not only frees us to ask but in a larger sense commands us to be seekers. When an honest question about faith—or about anything else, for that matter—rises within us, Jesus tells us to go ahead and fuss with it. Of course, the tough part in questioning is discerning at what point we should simply accept our present knowledge as sufficient or continue to ponder.

The important thing at this point is that God in Christ Jesus validates human "knocking"; more than this, by implication, God validates the circumstances that bring about knocking. I don't know about you, but most of my questioning has taken place during difficult times. When days are chugging by in fine fashion, I may ponder the mysteries of existence, but I do so leisurely and without anxiety. But when I'm in the middle of a crisis, my searching has voltage to it. I knock loudly.

Matthew 7:7–11 lets me know that God expects me to behave in this way. This being the case, God must also recognize that crises are to be expected. I sometimes catch myself living under the illusion that if I can be a good enough Christian, I will function like Jesus did most of the time, calmly falling asleep as the ship pitches in the storm. Although this is a fine aspiration, it's also important to recall that Jesus threw himself on the ground in the garden of Gethsemane. Jesus did ask, search, and knock. We, like him, will also have moments when we feel peaceful in the midst of suffering and challenge. In a sense, God blesses our turmoil, validates it, by telling us how to respond. After all, we would have no need of the command to ask, search, and knock if we didn't have the crises that create in us the longing for answers.

And we are promised answers, but the promise isn't simple and pat: "For everyone who asks receives, and everyone who searches finds, and for everyone who knocks, the door will be opened." Jesus doesn't say exactly what the asker, searcher, and knocker will get, only that the asker receives, that the searcher finds, and that the door will be opened for the one who knocks. The key here is that the process of seeking will be rewarded, not that the specific question will be answered or the particular request granted. We can easily read this passage as suggesting that we should expect to get exactly what we ask for, but if we embrace a larger vision of Jesus' teaching, we might find at least the beginning of an answer. The question is, What does God hear when I pray? Does God hear, "Please don't let my mother die"? Or does God hear some more profound petition that I can't articulate? Maybe God understands the request on my lips to be far from the need of my heart.

There aren't answers to these questions. All I can say is that when I reflect on my own prayers in the midst of struggle and uncertainty, I discover in hindsight that God responded not to what I asked for but to what I needed. Long ago, I figured that what I needed most was more control over my time so that I could get more writing done. Committee meetings and piles of papers awaiting grades seemed to fill each day. I wouldn't exactly say that I "prayed" to God for more hours in the day or fewer professional responsibilities, but I did look toward the heavens now and again and sigh loudly. Fortunately, God addressed my sigh, not my perceived need. Instead of lavishing money or spare time upon me, God gave me children. God is not without a sense of humor. One of the many lessons I learned from having kids is that far from needing more control over my time and everything else, what I need is to admit how little in my life I'm able to control and how that's probably for the best, given that God is the one in charge. Like everyone else, I still have lots of days when I wish I could dictate how things would go for me, but during my period of greatest wondering and struggling, I asked, searched, and knocked. And in time, I got some answers. The thing was, the answers I got (Elena and Micah first among them) were to questions I didn't have the smarts to ask.

At the time of my uncertainty, I didn't know that Jesus commands us to ask, search, and knock. I hadn't studied Greek yet. If the truth be told, I don't know that I would have cared back then. I certainly didn't know that what I was going through could in any way be considered holy, and that my reaction to suffering was faithful. This much I do know: had I not wrestled with the mystery, I certainly wouldn't be writing this book right now.

Invitation to Reflection

- In Genesis 32, Jacob wrestled with a stranger all night long, "until daybreak." When the stranger asked Jacob to release him, Jacob said, "I will not let you go, unless you bless me." At the end of the story, Jacob learned that he'd been wrestling with God. I don't know where we get the idea that God is unapproachable, for Scripture has many examples of faithful folks wrestling with God. Consider for a moment the possibility that God may be inviting us to a divine grappling match. How does this notion sit with your understanding of faithfulness?

- I once told an elderly man whose best friend was dying that it was okay to be mad at God. He thanked me but then said, "But I'd be mad even if you hadn't said I could." He was way ahead of me. Have you ever been angry with God? If so, how did you work your way through that?

- What sort of asking, searching, and knocking have you done in your own life? Can you think of ways that God has answered your prayers in unexpected ways?

The Grand Illusion

¹ Then Jesus was led up by the Spirit into the wilderness to be tempted by the devil. ² He fasted forty days and forty nights, and afterwards he was famished. ³ The tempter came and said to him, "If you are the Son of God, command these stones to become loaves of bread." ⁴ But he answered, "It is written,

'One does not live by bread alone,

> but by every word that comes from the mouth
> of God.'"

⁵ Then the devil took him to the holy city and placed him on the pinnacle of the temple, ⁶ saying to him, "If you are the Son of God, throw yourself down; for it is written,

'He will command his angels concerning you,'

> and 'On their hands they will bear you up,
> so that you will not dash your foot against a stone.'"

7Jesus said to him, "Again it is written, 'Do not put the Lord your God to the test.'"

8Again, the devil took him to a very high mountain and showed him all the kingdoms of the world and their splendor; 9and he said to him, "All these will I give you, if you will fall down and worship me." 10Jesus said to him, "Away with you, Satan! for it is written,

'Worship the Lord your God, and serve only him.'"

11Then the devil left him, and suddenly angels came and waited on him.

❧ ❧ ❧

THE UNEXPECTED TEACHING:
Jesus was tempted to purchase the grand illusion.

In *Invitation to Love,* Father Thomas Keating presents a useful and valid interpretation of Satan's temptation of Jesus and the meaning of Jesus' refusal. Keating notes that we human beings have three central needs that grow out of what he calls our "false self," which he defines as "the self developed in our own likeness rather than in the likeness of God." This false self gets us into all sorts of trouble by seducing us into thinking that we'll be happy if only we're able to satisfy our desire for control, security, and esteem.

According to Keating, the three temptations Jesus faced were directed at these needs of the false self. When Satan said, "Are you hungry? Make bread from these stones," he was attacking Jesus' human desire to control matters in his life. All Jesus needed to do was take control from God and rely on his own wisdom. His response was astute: "I'll let God decide what I need. God is my food."

Next, Satan took Jesus up to the pinnacle of the temple and said, "Jump and let angels catch you." The suggestion was transparent. Jesus should jump and let angels snag him at the last second. Then everyone in town would witness the miracle and crowd around him and say, "Okay, you're our man." Jesus saw right through the ploy: "I'm the Son of God already. I don't have to pass your test to prove it. I don't need you to throw me a 'coming out' party." In other words, Jesus' sense of esteem was just fine, thank you.

Satan's third temptation is actually kind of funny. He wanted to give Jesus all the kingdoms of the world. Nice try. Rather like me giving away my neighbor Gary's big shiny black truck. Ain't mine to give. The bait in this case was security. If Jesus owned the whole world, he'd have no worries. He'd never have to complain about not having a place to lay his head. He'd be able to do that any place he liked—if only he'd worship Satan. Jesus knew that he was being offered manure here. Worshiping the devil would be a lie, for Jesus wouldn't really believe in what he was doing anyway; what's more, he would be purchasing something, the kingdoms of the world, that wouldn't give him real security anyway.

How do we apply this story to our own lives? Through his temptation, Jesus demonstrated that we live under the illusion that anything but God can satisfy our souls' needs. He also revealed the futility of control, security, and approval, and suggested that achieving them won't supply us with the feeling of peace and contentment we're longing for.

Careers are a good example of this phenomenon. If we look at the trajectory of just about any career, advancement is marked by ever higher wages and increasing numbers of subordinates. The arrow is always pointing upward. More money, more people to supervise. Fine performance is rewarded with financial wealth, which helps us to control our own lives, and authority, which helps us to control the lives of others. The assumption is that moving up the ladder will feed our need for control, security, and esteem—and society praises the extent to which we are fed in this way.

The problem with these needs is that they're bottomless. No matter how much money one has, how many underlings, how much applause, it's never enough. And so we crowd ourselves with what we assume will satisfy that appetite: positions of leadership, slick and expensive toys, folks who tell us we're swell. And our hunger never goes away.

Then, at some point, when we're thirty, forty, fifty, older yet, our lives come to crisis. Some folks put words to their misery, and those words usually say something like, "Is this all there is?" Others grit their teeth and plow ahead, hoping somehow that the fog of longing will lift from their lives. Sometimes it does, and sometimes it doesn't.

There's nothing new here. Henry David Thoreau said pretty much the same thing in *Walden:* "The mass of men lead lives of quiet desperation." Peace and contentment, which is not always to say happiness, come from a detachment from control, security, and esteem. Because the world is caught up in satisfying the false self, folks who attempt to let go of the false self and its lies seem odd. Maybe they wear baggy, unfashionable clothes. Maybe they're very quiet. Maybe they take a big pay cut and change jobs for reasons nobody quite understands. Or maybe, like Thoreau, they spend some time living alone in the woods.

I can imagine such people walking next to Jesus—wandering is more like it. They would travel light. People would laugh at them, call them aimless. Their feet would be dirty, but that would be okay. Jesus, to whom they had given all, including their assumptions about joy, would wash their feet. They would have little, but their hearts would sing. They would have no false sense of control, security, or esteem—and no illusions. Each day would be a new attempt to let go of lies, the lies told by the hoarding of things and people. Each moment, full of celebration or despair or both, would welcome the radical freedom of Jesus, who said, "One does not live by bread alone, but by every word that comes from the mouth of God."

Invitation to Reflection

٭ As you reflect on issues of control, security, and esteem in your own life, what stands out? Are there any areas that seem out of balance? Is there within you either anxiety or bottomless longing that might be attached to one of these needs?

* It certainly isn't easy to detach ourselves from basic, earthly needs. One way to approach the need for control, security, and esteem is to focus simply on the need for control. To what extent do you control the circumstances of your life? How do you feel when events arise over which you have no control? How do you manage in such situations?

* Consider for a moment major figures in the Bible. If you aren't familiar with the Bible, think perhaps of people you regard as models of faith. As you recall their stories, how much control, security, and esteem did they possess? What might we all learn from their faith journeys?

The RESTORATIVE

TEACHINGS

"Then the woman left her water jar and went back to the city. She said to the people, 'Come and see a man who told me everything I have ever done! He cannot be the Messiah, can he?'" (JOHN 4:28–29)

TRUTH IN THE
TERRIFYING CLOUD

Luke 9:28–36

²⁸*Now about eight days after these sayings Jesus took with him
Peter and John and James, and went up on the mountain to
pray.* ²⁹*And while he was praying, the appearance of his face
changed, and his clothes became dazzling white.* ³⁰*Suddenly
they saw two men, Moses and Elijah, talking to him.* ³¹*They
appeared in glory and were speaking of his departure, which he
was about to accomplish at Jerusalem.* ³²*Now Peter and his
companions were weighed down with sleep; but since they had
stayed awake, they saw his glory and the two men who stood
with him.* ³³*Just as they were leaving him, Peter said to Jesus,
"Master, it is good for us to be here; let us make three dwellings,
one for you, one for Moses, and one for Elijah"—not knowing
what he said.* ³⁴*While he was saying this, a cloud came and
overshadowed them; and they were terrified as they entered the
cloud.* ³⁵*Then from the cloud came a voice that said, "This is*

my Son, my Chosen; listen to him!" *36When the voice had spo-*
ken, Jesus was found alone. And they kept silent and in those
days told no one any of the things they had seen.

❦ ❦ ❦

The Unexpected Teaching:
Peter clogged up the moment.

I was walking in the woods with a friend when we
came upon a large inlet of water framed by enormous
pines. The sky was so deeply blue I wanted to fall into it
and bite the few absolutely white clouds.

So we stood on this shore, my friend and I, in
silence. Then he said, "Ah, I just want to drink this in."

Ah, I thought to myself, *I just want to bip you on
the nose!*

He'd clogged up the moment. Of course, I didn't
really get mad at him. We all have our quota of awkward
things we have to say and do in a lifetime, and this was
just one more that he could get out of the way when not
too many people were around.

Because Peter's words and deeds are recorded in
Scripture, we get to check his "oops" quota, and what
Peter said in this transfiguration account, in which Jesus'
postresurrection glory is made visible, is a little-known
item on his list. Imagine the majesty of the moment.
Jesus, Moses, and Elijah had just been together. This
topped any get-together we can imagine. Better than a
reunion of the Beatles. Better than Babe Ruth, Hank

Aaron, and Mark McGwire in the batting lineup together. Jesus' clothes were "dazzling white," his face mysteriously transformed. Then just as Moses and Elijah were waving good-bye, Peter said, "Uh, how about I pitch a tent?" Almost as if to cover up his words, a cloud "overshadowed" them, and God spoke.

Bip!

Like I said, we all do the kind of thing Peter did. The question is, Why? What is it about profound moments that bring out the dingbat in us? My guess is, we find ourselves actually afraid because we know that we have drawn close to the divine—or more accurately, the divine One has drawn close to us. And so rather than just exist in that moment when we sense God with us in a unique way, we say or do something weird or inappropriate in hopes of relieving our tension. The presence of God was overwhelming for Peter. I have to wonder if God's words near the end of this passage, "This is my Son, my Chosen; listen to him!" wasn't God's way of saying, "Peter, shut up and just pay attention." Peter said something to deal with his own anxiety or excitement, not to contribute something meaningful to the moment.

If wonderful experiences threaten to turn us into momentary dopes, profoundly difficult experiences are even worse. And here, I have no intention to be humorous. When I worked as a chaplain in a hospital for a short time, I often saw how the temptation to clog up moments is excruciating when people are sick or dying. As the person who would come on the scene in hopes of bringing comfort, I would often want to say, "Now, now, everything will be okay. You'll see," or "You need to have faith." Friends and family members would often say such things to each other. What I learned from some very wise teachers and colleagues, however, is that sometimes we speak words of comfort to relieve ourselves of the stress we feel, not to offer genuine help to a sufferer. And saying, "You're going to be fine" to a kid whose mother is dying isn't only clogging up a moment, it's also not true. The kid, in this case, is going to grieve and struggle for a long time. In the end, this reality can be too much for us to face, so we say something to deny the profound closeness of the truth. Gandhi said, "God is truth." Maybe God, like truth, can be tough to take. Both set us free, but seldom do we come away from the encounter wearing a button with a smiley face on it.

One of the hardest things I've ever done was sit and hold the hand of a man who was going to die—and not to say stupid stuff, just to let his dying hours be his dying hours, to witness something sacred without either giving play-by-play commentary or otherwise filling the silence by bumping my gums together.

Peter meant well. I've meant well when I've made noise to ease my anxiety at touching God. We all mean well. The point is, both lovely and difficult moments are gifts from God. Those gifts stand on their own, "far above our poor powers to add or detract," as Abraham Lincoln said of the Battle of Gettysburg. Often when we speak, we say far more about our own feelings than about the gifts of what surrounds us.

Still, we all have that quota to meet. Sometimes, we deserve to be bipped, but always we receive forgiveness.

Invitation to Reflection

- One way to think about clogging up special moments is to pay attention to silence. As a culture, we are uncomfortable with stillness and quiet. How comfortable are you with silence? Are you able to let seconds go by without saying something just to fill the air with noise?
- Can you think of situations in which you or others have done things for no other reason than to reduce anxiety? What is it about such situations, as best you can figure, that makes us uneasy?
- Sit in a comfortable position, close your eyes, and try to rest your mind for five minutes. Relax and regard ideas that come to you as boats floating by as you sit on the bank of a river. You are aware that the boats are moving past you, but you're not focusing on them. After the five minutes, reflect about how your body felt during this time and what kinds of thoughts came to you. Did you feel like you wanted to get up and do something? Or were you able to rest in silence?

To Befriend
the Mystery

John 7:25–31

²⁵*Now some of the people of Jerusalem were saying, "Is not this the man whom they are trying to kill?* ²⁶*And here he is, speaking openly, but they say nothing to him! Can it be that the authorities really know that this is the Messiah?* ²⁷*Yet we know where this man is from; but when the Messiah comes, no one will know where he is from."* ²⁸*Then Jesus cried out as he was teaching in the temple, "You know me, and you know where I am from. I have not come on my own. But the one who sent me is true, and you do not know him.* ²⁹*I know him, because I am from him, and he sent me."* ³⁰*Then they tried to arrest him, but no one laid hands on him, because his hour had not yet come.* ³¹*Yet many in the crowd believed in him and were saying, "When the Messiah comes, will he do more signs than this man has done?"*

❦ ❦ ❦

The Unexpected Teaching:
Jesus lived within God's time frame.

A couple of years after I graduated from college, a classmate of mine, Ken, was diagnosed with lymphoma and died within six weeks. He was living across the country from me, and we'd fallen out of touch. I got a call one day and learned Ken was sick and at the point of trying some carrot-juice therapy, so I figured things were bad. Two days later, I got the call that he was dead. Ken was twenty-three.

Flip side: a guy I used to know named Bob had emphysema. He was in his early seventies, and when I'd visit, it was all his gaunt chest could do to suck in enough air to keep going. Caught in a maddening tension—wanting to die because of the physical agony of fighting for each breath and wanting to live for fear of death—he talked of "doing something foolish" even as his eyes widened in panic when he couldn't breathe. Yet on he lived, sitting alone, waiting for his time to come.

Most of us have stories like these to tell, stories of people who died before they'd gotten their living done or lived when all they were doing was dying. My guess is, our minds have long acknowledged the fact that we just don't know why people live for as long as they do and die when and how they do. It's our hearts that struggle to accept God's time frame.

Once, I was visiting a woman in the hospital who was depressed about her declining health. "Why?" she said, looking at me through tears. "Why is this happening to me?" I made the mistake of thinking she was asking why with her brain when it was her heart asking the question. I didn't realize at the time that no language of words could speak to the why of the heart.

We humans like to think we know lots about this world, but we don't know. In this passage from John, how was it that no one laid hands on Jesus to arrest him? Maybe there was a reality operating in creation more profound and forceful than "hands" of the many people surrounding him in the temple. Why did Ken die at twenty-three with only six weeks' warning? Why did my old buddy Bob keep living when it was a herculean task just to make it to the bathroom? There's no way to know.

The temptation is to respond to such mysteries by saying sweet but dumb things, to try somehow to soothe the heart by talking to the head. In the midst of the staggering mystery of our living and dying, sometimes shutting up is the best option. Our hearts will always ask why, but maybe we can take the edge off our questioning by trying to befriend the mystery. It's hard, never quite knowing where the finish line is, but the realization that we can try to let go, to surrender to God's time frame, can give us a measure of peace, even as we long for answers.

Invitation to Reflection

✗ Try to think of an event in your life that has never been resolved. As you recall this event, what feelings come to you? Are you able to live peacefully with a lack of closure? Do the words "I don't know" flow easily from your mouth, or do you struggle to say them? Do you find it difficult to admit that there are things you don't know?

✶ Befriending mysteries is a rare and precious ability, but it's not unlike living with experiences that have never been resolved. Being able to rest easily in the midst of ambiguity and the unknown can be as elusive as not noticing the sound of a water faucet dripping in the night. Where are you now in your ability to sit comfortably with huge questions that won't be answered until God whispers into your ears? And can you let the faucet keep on dripping?

FRONT-PORCH MIRACLE

John 4:1–42

¹Now when Jesus learned that the Pharisees had heard, "Jesus is making and baptizing more disciples than John ² —although it was not Jesus himself but his disciples who baptized— ³he left Judea and started back to Galilee. ⁴But he had to go through Samaria. ⁵So he came to a Samaritan city called Sychar, near the plot of ground that Jacob had given to his son Joseph. ⁶Jacob's well was there, and Jesus, tired out by his journey, was sitting by the well. It was about noon.

⁷A Samaritan woman came to draw water, and Jesus said to her, "Give me a drink." ⁸(His disciples had gone to the city to buy food.) ⁹The Samaritan woman said to him, "How is it that you, a Jew, ask a drink of me, a woman of Samaria?" (Jews do not share things in common with Samaritans.) ¹⁰Jesus answered her, "If you knew the gift of God, and who it is that is saying to you, 'Give me a drink,' you would have asked him, and he would have given you living water." ¹¹The woman said to him, "Sir, you have no bucket, and the well is deep. Where do you get that living water? ¹²Are you greater than our ancestor Jacob, who gave us the well, and with his sons and his flocks drank from it?" ¹³Jesus said to her, "Everyone who drinks of this water will be thirsty again, ¹⁴but those who drink of the water that I will give them will never be thirsty. The water that I will give will become in them a spring of water gushing up to eternal life." ¹⁵The woman said to him, "Sir, give me this water, so that I may never be thirsty or have to keep coming here to draw water."

¹⁶Jesus said to her, "Go, call your husband, and come back." ¹⁷The woman answered him, "I have no husband." Jesus said to her, "You are right in saying, 'I have no husband'; ¹⁸for you have had five husbands, and the one you have now is not your husband. What you have said is true!" ¹⁹The woman said to him, "Sir, I see that you are a prophet. ²⁰Our ancestors worshiped on this mountain, but you say that the place where people must worship is in Jerusalem." ²¹Jesus said to her, "Woman, believe me, the hour is coming when you will worship the Father neither on this mountain nor in Jerusalem. ²²You worship what you do not know; we worship what we know, for salvation is from the Jews. ²³But the hour is coming, and is now here, when the true worshipers will worship the Father in spirit and truth, for the Father seeks such as these to worship him. ²⁴God is spirit, and those who worship him must worship in spirit and truth." ²⁵The woman said to him, "I

know that Messiah is coming (who is called Christ). When he comes, he will proclaim all things to us." [26]Jesus said to her, "I am he, the one who is speaking to you."

[27]Just then his disciples came. They were astonished that he was speaking with a woman, but no one said, "What do you want?" or, "Why are you speaking with her?" [28]Then the woman left her water jar and went back to the city. She said to the people, [29]"Come and see a man who told me everything I have ever done! He cannot be the Messiah, can he?" [30]They left the city and were on their way to him.

[31]Meanwhile the disciples were urging him, "Rabbi, eat something." [32]But he said to them, "I have food to eat that you do not know about." [33]So the disciples said to one another, "Surely no one has brought him something to eat?" [34]Jesus said to them, "My food is to do the will of him who sent me and to complete his work. [35]Do you not say, 'Four months more, then comes the harvest'? But I tell you, look around you, and see how the fields are ripe for harvesting. [36]The reaper is already receiving wages and is gathering fruit for eternal life, so that sower and reaper may rejoice together. [37]For here the saying holds true, 'One sows and another reaps.' [38]I sent you to reap that for which you did not labor. Others have labored, and you have entered into their labor."

[39]Many Samaritans from that city believed in him because of the woman's testimony, "He told me everything I have ever done." [40]So when the Samaritans came to him, they asked him to stay with them; and he stayed there two days. [41]And many more believed because of his word. [42]They said to the woman, "It is no longer because of what you said that

we believe, for we have heard for ourselves, and we know that this is truly the Savior of the world."

❧ ❧ ❧

The Unexpected Teaching:
Jesus accepted the woman at the well just as she was.

I sometimes feel nostalgic about the middle-class neighborhood I grew up in during the sixties and seventies. The folks who lived on Wagner Avenue in Erie, Pennsylvania, were regular enough. We all had our allotment of human frailties and secrets of the heart. Still, everybody knew what was going on with everybody else, though nothing was said. In the summer, we'd sit with each other on front porches, eat food we didn't know was bad for us, and talk. Just talk. And after a while, I'd get bored and either go off to play with friends while the adults talked some more or practice kicking field goals over the telephone wire that was strung across the street.

What I remember most—admittedly through the soft glow of memory—is an unspoken acceptance that neighbor had for neighbor. Of course, this acceptance was fragile, so I don't want to push this picture. If an African American family had moved into the neighborhood, for example, I'm not sure they would have been welcome. I know the old gay guy who lived across the street wasn't really welcome; we were quietly told to steer clear of him. I also realize that sometimes what looked like compassion was mostly an effort to keep the boat steady. Even so, at our best moments, people in my neighborhood were good to each other, even though we knew the next-door neighbor's muck.

When we read that Jesus met the woman of Samaria at the well, our impulse is to marvel at another of his miracles. "Ah," we say, "he read her like a book. Her past and present were completely open to him. Jesus must have been the Messiah! Who else could have performed such a sign?" Impressive as this is, I don't think Jesus' divination of the facts of the woman's life is the heart of the miracle. Sure, divination is slick, but it's a red herring.

The real miracle in this story is that Jesus told the woman "everything she had ever done" but didn't criticize her shortcomings. In other words, he knew her and accepted her for who she was. For me, this acceptance is the miracle, not Jesus' omniscience. The woman said to Jesus, "When he [Messiah] comes, he will proclaim all things to us." And that's exactly what he did for her. He told her who she was.

This woman of Samaria, who wasn't even named in the story, whose conversation with Jesus was shocking to the disciples simply because of her gender and race, was important to Jesus. He sat and talked with her. At first glance, an exchange between a man and a woman doesn't seem remarkable, but in this case, it was. As Gail R. O'Day writes, Jesus "violates two societal conventions. First, a Jewish man did not initiate conversation with an unknown woman. Moreover, a Jewish teacher did not engage in public conversation with a woman. . . . Second, Jews did not invite contact with Samaritans." So this was no run-of-the-mill chat. Even in what appears to us commonplace, Jesus revealed his radical love.

Jesus' words to the Samaritan woman must have been both extensive and revealing. Her statement to the people of Sychar—"Come and see a man who told me everything I have ever done!"—may have been a stretch, but her encounter with Jesus probably made her feel as though he knew her through and through.

If we read into the story, we can imagine that the woman must have felt somehow affirmed, accepted, or loved by Jesus. If he had told her that she was a rotten little tramp, I don't suppose she would have gone back to the city, leaving her water jar behind at the well, and asked that pregnant question: "He cannot be the Messiah, can he?"

It would be misleading to say that Jesus didn't judge folks with stinging honesty when necessary. Ask any scribe or Pharisee. But in the story of the Samaritan woman, Jesus' gift to her was intimacy without condemnation. Given her reaction, we can only imagine the power and poignancy of the encounter for her.

People these days are ravenous for the miracle of intimacy that Jesus and the woman at the well shared. And there is something miraculous about being really known and affirmed by another human being. One time, I was sitting on a front porch, not on Wagner Avenue, with a friend who felt that our relationship had reached a point of closeness that he either had to share with me the fact that he was gay or accept a boundary in our friendship that didn't make him happy. So he told me. I'll never forget how nervous he was, how his hands, stuffed into his lap, were knit together as if in prayer. He knew me well enough to know that I wouldn't reject him, but . . . the danger of being known! We embraced, and I thanked him for trusting me and our friendship enough to tell me about this part of who he was. Then he relaxed. His arms and hands loosened up, and he was his old self again.

Or was he? It seems to me that both he and I were new people because of the miracle of intimacy. A whisper of trust and joy was granted us, for we caught an echo, just a hint in the breeze of that cool day, of what God's grace through Christ is like. It is sacred to have the secrets hiding in the bruised places of our hearts said out loud and to hear loving replies. John's Gospel contains many of Jesus' loving words: "I will come again and will take you to myself, so that where I am, you may be also" (14:3); "I will not leave you orphaned" (14:18); "As the Father has loved me, so I have loved you; abide in my love" (15:9).

Jesus knew the Twelve. He knew the woman of Samaria. He knows each of us, too, every little dusty cranny, and in our moment of greatest fear that we are too broken to be loved by God, we hear Jesus' voice: "Do not let your hearts be troubled, and do not let them be afraid" (John 14:27b).

Invitation to Reflection ✣

✣ I can remember my mom's endless conversations with other women in the neighborhood where I grew up. Now I recognize the spaciousness of what seemed at the time idle chatter. I think that thirty or forty years ago folks had time to talk to each other, to laugh, to enjoy the company of a friend or neighbor. What do you think about this? Is life too crowded these days for a cup of coffee and an hour's visit?

✣ Over the last few years, I've visited with quite a few homebound people. I bring them communion, and we simply share stories and thoughts. I've come to believe that the loneliness I so often see in them is a matter of being unknown, forgotten. What do you think lies at the source of loneliness? How can you reach out to those among you who might long for the knowing presence of another?

✣ Families and even faith communities suffer because their members don't have the energy to pay attention to each other. As your life currently stands, are you able to attend lovingly and generously to those around you? Is there intimacy in your life?

GRACE AND ONE TUNIC FOR THE JOURNEY

Luke 9:1–6

¹ Then Jesus called the twelve together and gave them power and authority over all demons and to cure diseases, ² and he sent them out to proclaim the kingdom of God and to heal. ³ He said to them, "Take nothing for your journey, no staff, nor bag, nor bread, nor money—not even an extra tunic. ⁴ Whatever house you enter, stay there, and leave from there. ⁵ Wherever they do not welcome you, as you are leaving that town shake the dust off your feet as a testimony against them." ⁶ They departed and went through the villages, bringing the good news and curing diseases everywhere.

❧ ❧ ❧

The Unexpected Teaching:

Jesus told his disciples to travel light.

We Christians have a way of reading the Bible that generally works to our advantage. We follow the commandments we like (or at least know we can't get out of), acquiesce to those that don't bother us, and shrug off those that strike us as outdated or politically incorrect. I'm speaking here of biblical injunctions, offered as such, either by Jesus or the many other faithful voices in the Old and New Testaments.

Another matter entirely are instructions or directives, especially those of Jesus to his disciples. These don't read exactly like commandments—maybe because Jesus didn't carry them down from a mountain chiseled into stone. For example, in Matthew 10:32, Jesus tells the Twelve, "Everyone therefore who acknowledges me before others, I also will acknowledge before my Father in heaven, but whoever denies me before others, I also will deny before my Father in heaven." Now, these words aren't phrased as a command, exactly, but they may as well be. The same basic message also appears in Mark (8:38) and Luke (9:26). It's odd, therefore, that when we choose to talk about commandments, this particular injunction never seems to come up. If we obsess about the law, we tend to look upon our own weakness and not upon God's grace in Jesus Christ, as we ought, but were we to list other commandments beyond the ten, we would probably include, "Thou shalt not be ashamed of me."

Some words of qualification are in order here. As a Lutheran, I believe that my relationship with God doesn't rest on "shalts" and "shalt nots," but on the saving action of Jesus Christ. In him, I am put right with God and need not fret about God's faithfulness to me in the present and future. This being said, as I try to accept God's grace and as I discern God's will for me in this time and place, I seek guidance about how I ought to live. I do so not out of fear that I'll be roasted on a spit for all eternity if I don't but out of gratefulness, a desire to care for all that God has made, and an awareness that God's will—as it finds voice in Scripture, my community of faith, and my own prayer and reflection—is my best shot at contentment. I realize that my own wisdom is inadequate, and sometimes downright toxic, for the nurturing of my spiritual, physical, and mental health. And so I seek out God's word, most powerfully spoken by Jesus, as I try to navigate this world. There is an invitational quality about Jesus' instructions. If I want to live in ways that will bring me wholeness and well-being, I listen. If I want to engage in constant frustration and disappointment, I do as I please. It's my choice.

Such is the case with Jesus' instructions to his disciples in this passage, as he sent them out to do the work of the kingdom of God. They were told, in effect, to travel light on their journey. It seems likely to me that part of Jesus' goal here was that the Twelve entrust themselves to their hosts, allow people to offer them the gift of hospitality, and build relationships. At the same time, the phrasing implies more than that. To take nothing but the tunic on one's back was really to travel light.

I can see asking the men not to take a staff, which was a weapon as well as a walking stick. But what was the harm in taking along a little bread or money? And why not an extra tunic? It wasn't as though a tunic, bread, and some coins would have been particularly burdensome to carry.

The point in such extreme directives was to make clear that absolutely nothing other than God's love was of any use to the Twelve. No staff could protect them. No bag could contain what they needed. No bread or meat could feed them. No money could grease the skids of their journey. No extra tunic could make them feel clean or comfortable. God alone would provide.

For us, the question is, What does "no staff, nor bag, nor bread, nor money—not even an extra tunic" mean for Christians today? If we look to Jesus for wisdom in living as healthy disciples, we wonder what he would tell us to take or not take for our journey. Here, I can only say how I have begun to discern this matter for myself. What Luke 9:1–6 says to me is that habitual, daily, material extravagance is not in harmony with God's will. If I concern myself with obtaining and maintaining the opulence that I can acquire by my own skill or cleverness, I unwittingly turn my back on the radiance of God's love, which is given to me for free. And because material possessions can distract me from God's grace, they have within them at least the potential to be lying scoundrels. I'm mindful, therefore, of what I buy and even hope for. Do I want a suitable car, for example, because I legitimately want to ride in safety and comfort? If so, no problem. But if I want the Mercedes or

BMW, or even the sport utility vehicle, because I suppose a fine ride will quiet my furious longing for God's presence, then heaven help me. I will have sunk thousands of bucks into a one-night stand. And when I hear of a person who won millions in the lottery, am I envious because I believe that those riches will at long last bring peace to my spirit?

My own calling is to live in awareness of the assumptions of my heart and spirit, to know why I want what I want. Like all of us, I sometimes live in a great cloud of wishes, disoriented, reaching for something I can't quite find. When all I can think about is where my extra tunic is, I can see neither the real blessings before me nor my brothers and sisters who need to experience God's grace. All I can think about is my tunic.

Even an extra tunic! If I think for an instant that a tunic will fill the spot in me reserved for God in Christ Jesus, I'm putting it back on the rack.

Invitation to Reflection ꙮ

✶ The Bible can be used to support scads of opinions—among them, the viewpoint that it's okay to have gobs of money and possessions. One can defend such a position with Scripture. Where do you stand on this issue? Is a life of Christian discipleship compatible with a life of luxury? Is Jesus' command to travel light for us as well as for the disciples? Either way, try to work through your position on this subject.

- Christians often use the word *idolatry* to refer to those things in life that we try to substitute for God: work, money, power, appearance, sex, food, and drugs are a few common fill-ins for God. Most of the time, we're not even aware we're engaged in idolatry. Can you see things in your own life that you worship in place of the Lord?

- As any traveler knows, packing light can be liberating. Think of times in your life when you've gone without something and been the better for it. Is it true to say that, in many cases, extra baggage is an extra burden?

CALLINGS

John 15:1–17

1 "I am the true vine, and my Father is the vinegrower. 2 He removes every branch in me that bears no fruit. Every branch that bears fruit he prunes to make it bear more fruit. 3 You have already been cleansed by the word that I have spoken to you. 4 Abide in me as I abide in you. Just as the branch cannot bear fruit by itself unless it abides in the vine, neither can you unless you abide in me. 5 I am the vine, you are the branches. Those who abide in me and I in them bear much fruit, because apart from me you can do nothing. 6 Whoever does not abide in me is thrown away like a branch and withers; such branches are gathered, thrown into the fire, and burned. 7 If you abide in me, and my words abide in you, ask for whatever you wish, and it will be done for you. 8 My Father is glorified by this, that you bear much fruit and become my disciples. 9 As the Father has loved me, so I have loved you; abide in my love. 10 If you keep my commandments, you will abide in my love, just as I have kept my Father's commandments and abide in his love. 11 I have said these things to you so that my joy may be in you, and that your joy may be complete.

12 "This is my commandment, that you love one another as I have loved you. 13 No one has greater love than this, to lay down one's life for one's friends. 14 You are my friends if you do what I command you. 15 I do not call you servants any longer, because the servant does not know what the master is doing; but I have called you friends, because I have made known to you everything that I have heard from my Father. 16 You did not choose me but I chose you. And I appointed you to go and bear fruit, fruit that will last, so that the Father will give you whatever you ask him in my name. 17 I am giving you these commands so that you may love one another."

❧ ❧ ❧

THE UNEXPECTED TEACHING:
The disciples didn't choose themselves;
they were chosen by God.

Autonomy. I love to think I'm autonomous, that I'm in control of my life, that I make wise and balanced choices about everything from the coffee I drink to the books I read, from the rules I expect my kids to obey to the religious beliefs I embrace. The older I get, however, and the more I learn and reflect, the more I see how much I'm guided by forces I don't always understand or recognize. Decisions I used to regard (when I was aware of them at all) as moments of autonomy, I now see as lenses on who I am, what has shaped my personality, and how unaware I often am about the reasons for my actions.

Take coffee—a small matter, of course. When I was in college, I took a course on the poetry of John Milton. There were just a few of us enrolled, so John, the professor, asked if we wanted to meet off campus. Pam volunteered her place, so once a week for three or four hours we met at Pam's flat. Every class, somebody brought a snack, and John brought a great coffee, Commonwealth Blend. Pam brewed it strong. And so we sat in a circle, talked about *Paradise Lost, Paradise Regained, Comus,* and so on, drank some wicked coffee, and chewed on bread and cheese. This was the first little community of friends I became part of as an adult, and I'll never forget the feeling of being new to this small group of English majors, yet taken in, fed, nourished, accepted, challenged. I found grace among these folks that's still fresh for me. I came to them as a bright enough kid but also as unsophisticated and racist in ways I couldn't yet see. These people gave me the chance to grow out of my mistakes without exactly letting me get away with them. Once, before class, I told a joke about blacks and watermelons. John looked away and said, half to me and half under his breath, "That's not funny." I knew right away that I'd crossed some line, and as weeks and months went by, I slowly figured out why my joke wasn't funny.

Anyway, the cup of hazelnut I just polished off five or six sentences ago was bought, freshly ground, and brewed mostly because of that group of friends. Now, it's true that coffee is no big deal, and I don't get quite this caught up in analyzing the reasons for every product I buy. Still, it matters that something as simple as the kind of java I drink is influenced by an experience of community that I certainly wasn't responsible for generating, not by my own pristine autonomy.

It's a scary reality that all decisions work this same way. We think we govern ourselves, but really all our experiences and relationships guide us in ways we can only begin to fathom. It's valid to say, in fact, that we are our experiences and relationships, or at least we are what we do with them. And, again, our every action and belief, from buying coffee to raising our kids, is all wrapped up together with our identities and characters. I believe, for example, that I shouldn't judge other people. I didn't just think that belief up. For years, I watched my mom frequently refuse to grind folks into the ground with words. She'd had some disappointments in her own life, and it was to her credit that she turned them into an ability to understand and exercise patience with others. In a sense, then, my belief about judging others was given to me.

Another way of saying the same thing is that I was called to a belief. Some beliefs to which I am called, because of my experiences and relationships, aren't very healthy or helpful, and I do well to neglect them. Others are wise and sacred, so I'm well served by embracing them.

In this passage from John, when Jesus tells the Twelve, "You did not choose me but I chose you," he's lifting up the idea that the disciples didn't just think up following Jesus, but he chose them or called them. They didn't personally have the power or wherewithal to leave their catches of fish behind on the beach and follow him. It's easy to imagine that they felt an attraction they couldn't explain, a certainty about who Jesus was that pulled them along behind him. The call they were hearing somehow felt right, even though it seemed foolish, maybe dangerous.

This image of call is central to our identity as Christians, and here's why. On the surface, the story of Jesus' life and death doesn't make much sense. For one thing, there are as many belief systems and theologies as there are cultures in this world. Why should this one be the right one? Also, why should we believe that some wise man two thousand years ago was the Son of God? Most of all, what sense does it make that Jesus should be tortured and killed and that this wretched event could mean redemption for humanity?

As I sit here, thinking through the beliefs I claim, part of me says, *It's Marx's opium, John. You believe this stuff so as not to be knocked unconscious from despair.* What I'm aware of most powerfully these days is that I don't confess Jesus as Savior because it makes sense but because I'm called to believe it. Martin Luther made this point in his *Small Catechism:*

> I believe that by my own understanding or strength I cannot believe in Jesus Christ my Lord or come to him, but instead the Holy Spirit has called me through the Gospel, enlightened me with his gifts, made me holy, and kept me in the true faith, just as he calls, gathers, enlightens, and makes holy the whole Christian church on earth

and keeps it with Jesus Christ in the one common, true faith. Daily in the Christian church the Holy Spirit abundantly forgives all sins—mine and those of all believers. On the last day the Holy Spirit will raise me and all the dead, and will give to me and all believers in Christ eternal life. This is most certainly true.

What Jesus taught in John 15:1–17 and Luther wrote about in the *Small Catechism* both point to this slippery truth: Christians are called to discipleship, called to bear fruit, called to believe.

More often than I would care to admit, the Thomas in me whispers, *Can all of this be true? It just doesn't add up, doesn't make sense. Am I only kidding myself?* Theologian Renita Weems once said pretty much this same thing in a sermon when she confessed to difficult periods of God's silence in her life. At such times, belief was almost out of reach, and then, she said, "I believe in believing." This is another way of confessing how dependent she is (and I know I am) on the Holy Spirit for giving her a belief in Jesus Christ as Lord. Some days, I find myself crying out, like the man in Mark's Gospel with a spirit-possessed boy, "I believe; help my unbelief!" (Mark 9:24).

At such moments, I try to remember who and whose I am. I'm an amalgam of what I have lived, whom I have loved, and what I have been called to believe. I didn't choose any of this stuff, but it chose me. I didn't choose to follow Jesus, but in the Spirit Jesus called me. And so I follow him, some days quite closely, other days at some distance, longing to hear his voice, which calls me beyond logic, beyond my own good sense to the knowledge that saves me, but that—how odd!—I can't accept but for God's grace.

Invitation to Reflection ✿

✶ Being a Christian can seem a foolhardy adventure at times. No matter how hard we try to substantiate our faith with solid evidence, we simply can't prove that Jesus Christ is Lord. How do you feel about the fact that, in worldly terms, the Christian faith makes little sense? How do you talk to your friends about the faith to which you've been called?

✶ All the time I was growing up, my dad made it a point to reach out to friends of his whose loved ones died. From an early age, I went with Dad to the funeral home to pay respects. In this and in other ways, my dad taught me loyalty. I might even say that Dad called me to loyalty. To what beliefs, actions, and attitudes have you been called by those who love you?

✶ Those who work in the church often speak of their calling, a sense of trying to live out God's will for their lives. Reflect on what you believe God has called you to in life, or on what God might be calling you to in the future. This may be a career, but it need not be. Maybe you've been called to be a choir member, or a listening and compassionate presence in your neighborhood. God has as many callings as children.

GUARDIANS OF
GOD'S BELOVED

Luke 2:41–52

41 Now every year his parents went to Jerusalem for the festival of the Passover. 42 And when he was twelve years old, they went up as usual for the festival. 43 When the festival was ended and they started to return, the boy Jesus stayed behind in Jerusalem, but his parents did not know it. 44 Assuming that he was in the group of travelers, they went a day's journey. Then they started to look for him among their relatives and friends. 45 When they did not find him, they returned to Jerusalem to search for him. 46 After three days they found him in the temple, sitting among the teachers, listening to them and asking them questions. 47 And all who heard him were amazed at his understanding and his answers. 48 When his parents saw him they were astonished; and his mother said to him, "Child, why have you treated us like this? Look, your father and I have been searching for you in great anxiety." 49 He said to them, "Why were you searching for me? Did you not know that I must be in my Father's house?" [50]*But they did not understand what he said to them.* [51]*Then he went down with them and came to Nazareth, and was obedient to them. His mother treasured all these things in her heart.*

[52]*And Jesus increased in wisdom and in years, and in divine and human favor.*

✸ ✸ ✸

The Unexpected Teaching:
Mary and Joseph were guardians of a child of God.

I believe in the truth of Scripture, but I can't help but think this particular account of Jesus' boyhood has been, well, tidied up a bit. What did Mary do, for example, when she discovered after a day of travel that Jesus wasn't in tow? Did she have the nagging feeling that she forgot something? Did she suddenly slap her hands to her cheeks, bug out her eyes, and scream, very cinematically, "Jesus!"? And when she and Joseph finally tracked Jesus down, after four more days, did she really say the word *anxiety*? Or did she use a stronger word? And Joseph, what about him? If I'd been there, whether my son was the Messiah or not, I'd have said, "Where have you been, little man? Your mother and I were worried sick. What on earth were you thinking?"

As important as Joseph must have been in his son's life, Scripture doesn't tell us much about him. And for as crucial as Mary is to Christianity, she doesn't really get many lines in her script either. Why don't the parents of our Lord have larger parts to play in the accounts of Jesus' life and ministry? This story of the boy Jesus in the temple offers us an answer—one that we can apply to our lives today.

When his parents found him in the temple, Jesus said, "Did you not know I must be in my Father's house?" Note that he didn't say "God's house" or "the temple"; he said "my Father's house." We need to understand the impact of these words within the context of the story. Remember, Mary and Joseph had been all over creation looking for Jesus. When they found him at last, they were still beside themselves with the terror that rushes into the belly of any parent who contemplates losing a child. Jesus said to them, in the presence of lots of onlookers, "Hey, let's remember who my real parent is. It's God."

Jesus' statement was radical. He knew at twelve what adults can't seem to remember even when they have children or grandchildren: God is the primary parent of all. Human parents are simply blessed guardians. The distinction here is crucial to healthy parenting.

When we who are parents see ourselves as guardians entrusted with God's children, our understanding of parental responsibility ought to change radically. We no longer see our kids as possessions but as gifts that really belong to God. Assuming that we're taking reasonably good care of our children in the visible and expected ways (a big assumption in this world), knowing our kids as God's first and ours second should guide our actions and lower our stress. For example, suppose you've invited Jane, a coworker, John, her husband, and David, their five-year-old son, to your house for the evening. At the dinner table, David starts goofing around. You've told your own kids dozens of times not to mess around at the table, but David's messing. He's saying, "I like macaroni and cheese this much" and flinging his arms out wide. He does it again and again. Jane and John smile warmly. ("Isn't he cute?") About the eighth time, David knocks over his chocolate milk. His glass plops onto the butter plate. Brown tributaries rush in every direction. The question is, Would you holler at him? Probably not. Would you holler at your own kids? Probably. Why the difference? Because David's not your own kid, and his mother and father are sitting right there with you. It's amazing how you can be more restrained with someone else's child than with your own. If you shouted angrily at David, his parents would no doubt be offended. The comparison here is clear enough. Is God offended, disappointed, angered at witnessing the things parents do to their kids? And God does witness!

Of course, there is a reward to go along with the staggering responsibility of baby-sitting our Lord's children. As you watch your sons and daughters stomp through the minefields of childhood, adolescence, and puberty, you can find comfort in remembering that God loves your kids more than you ever could. When you let your ten-year-old son walk alone to the store for the first time, you know he's not really alone. When your fifteen-year-old daughter goes on her first date alone with a seventeen-year-old guy driving his dad's Infiniti,

God's in the back seat—perhaps tapping her on the shoulder at the appropriate (or inappropriate) moments. Even when your son wants to get married at twenty (too young as far as you're concerned), you know that God is closer to him than air, nearer than you can ever be. It's amazing to feel the peace of God when you can say, "God, I entrust to you what is your own—this child." Does this mean that bad things won't happen? Of course not. Look at what happened to Jesus as an adult. Things couldn't get more catastrophic than having your kid tortured, nailed to a cross, and left there naked and bleeding. Yet even this disaster was touched by grace. Jesus rose from the dead. We know, therefore, that nothing is beyond God's redemption. Bad things happen to our children, and sometimes we are responsible. Still, we stand in the presence of a dazzling mystery: in Jesus Christ, God enters into our failure and worry with us. Even as parents, we never stop being children of God, who loves us all more than we love our own children. When we cry, God cries. Earthly life offers no guarantee besides Jesus' words to his disciples: "I will not leave you orphaned" (John 14:18). As children of God and as guardians of God's children, we need to accept that promise.

Invitation to Reflection ✼

✼ How does God's ownership of everything in your life make decisions more complicated than they already are? How do the demands of God's ownership simplify decision making?

✘ In your life as an individual or as a member of a faith community, what parts of God's creation are most relevant to your responsibility as caretaker? What in your field of vision is crying out for your concern and attention?

✘ Once, my friend Chad and I were running in downtown Columbus, Ohio, when we came across a homeless guy dancing in circles. As we trotted by, it occurred to me that God loves the homeless guy as much as God loves me. We all belong to God. For a Christian, this is not simply a warm fuzzy observation. It has consequences. What might it mean for you that, regardless of your likes and dislikes, each person you encounter is beloved of God?

SOMETHING NEW
IN THE MANSION
OF THE LORD

John 20:11–18; 21:1–14

20 *¹¹But Mary stood weeping outside the tomb. As she wept,*
she bent over to look into the tomb; ¹²and she saw two angels
in white, sitting where the body of Jesus had been lying, one at
the head and the other at the feet. ¹³They said to her, "Woman,
why are you weeping?" She said to them, "They have taken
away my Lord, and I do not know where they have laid him."
¹⁴When she had said this, she turned around and saw Jesus
standing there, but she did not know that it was Jesus. ¹⁵Jesus
said to her, "Woman, why are you weeping? Whom are you
looking for?" Supposing him to be the gardener, she said to him,
"Sir, if you have carried him away, tell me where you have laid
him, and I will take him away." ¹⁶Jesus said to her, "Mary!"
She turned and said to him in Hebrew, "Rabbouni!" (which

means Teacher). *17 Jesus said to her, "Do not hold on to me, because I have not yet ascended to the Father. But go to my brothers and say to them, 'I am ascending to my Father and your Father, to my God and your God.'"* *18 Mary Magdalene went and announced to the disciples, "I have seen the Lord"; and she told them that he had said these things to her. . . .*

21 *1 After these things Jesus showed himself again to the disciples by the Sea of Tiberias; and he showed himself in this way.* *2 Gathered there were Simon Peter, Thomas called the Twin, Nathanael of Cana in Galilee, the sons of Zebedee, and two others of his disciples. 3 Simon Peter said to them, "I am going fishing." They said to him, "We will go with you." They went out and got into the boat, but that night they caught nothing.*

4 Just after daybreak, Jesus stood on the beach; but the disciples did not know that it was Jesus. 5 Jesus said to them, "Children, you have no fish, have you?" They answered him, "No." 6 He said to them, "Cast the net to the right side of the boat, and you will find some." So they cast it, and now they were not able to haul it in because there were so many fish. 7 That disciple whom Jesus loved said to Peter, "It is the Lord!" When Simon Peter heard that it was the Lord, he put on some clothes, for he was naked, and jumped into the sea. 8 But the other disciples came in the boat, dragging the net full of fish, for they were not far from the land, only about a hundred yards off.

9 When they had gone ashore, they saw a charcoal fire there, with fish on it, and bread. 10 Jesus said to them, "Bring some of the fish that you have just caught." 11 So Simon Peter went aboard and hauled the net ashore, full of large fish, a hundred fifty-three of them; and though there were so many, the net was not torn. *12 Jesus said to them, "Come and have breakfast." Now none of the disciples dared to ask him, "Who are you?" because they knew it was the Lord. 13 Jesus came and took the bread and gave it to them, and did the same with the fish. 14 This was now the third time that Jesus appeared to the disciples after he was raised from the dead.*

❦ ❦ ❦

THE UNEXPECTED TEACHING:
Mary and the disciples didn't recognize the risen Jesus.

I admit to being moved by John's postresurrection accounts more than those of the other Gospel writers. In John 20 and 21, the moments Jesus shared with his friends were intimate, actually continuations of the relationships they had already forged before his death on the cross. The love they all had for one another was obvious. All Jesus said was, "Mary!" and she knew immediately who was speaking. And when Peter realized who was standing on the beach, he put clothes on and jumped into the sea (a little puzzling, but never mind) to get to Jesus. They thought their lives were in the sewer, maybe that all they'd learned and experienced was a bunch of rubbish. But then he appeared to them, ate with them, spent a bit of time with them.

As much as those close to Jesus loved and needed him, they didn't recognize him at first after the resurrection. Only when Jesus spoke Mary's name and performed the miracle of full nets for the disciples did they realize who Jesus was. Luke's Gospel explains that the two disciples to whom Jesus appeared on the road to Emmaus didn't know who he was because "their eyes were kept from recognizing him" (Luke 24:16).

In John's Gospel, though, there is no such claim. They simply didn't know who Jesus was at first. Only after reestablishing their relationship with him did they perceive their Lord. We should fess up that there is tension between Luke's and John's postresurrection accounts, and what's at stake is of consequence. Luke's Gospel implies that the risen Jesus was the same as he'd always been but that God prevented the two disciples on the road from seeing him clearly. John's Gospel, on the other hand, implies that there was something significantly different about Jesus after he rose from the dead. At least he looked different enough that those who loved him mistook him for a stranger.

Distance might explain why the guys in the boat didn't recognize Jesus. After all, he was about a hundred yards away onshore; nevertheless, something was different. "Now none of the disciples dared to ask him, 'Who are you?' because they knew it was the Lord." Yes, they knew it was the Lord, but they were still tempted to ask, "Who are you?" He did rise from the tomb, and this was not exactly a commonplace occurrence. But why would the issue of Jesus' identity be in play at all, unless he was radically changed? In Mary Magdalene's case, there were no excuses. She and Jesus were standing face-to-face. But then he said her name. His looks may have been unfamiliar, but there was something about the way he said "Mary!" that touched her deeply.

The question is, What exactly does it mean that Jesus rose bodily from the dead, that he had a mouth through which to speak Mary's name and arms to receive her embrace? And what does it mean that he was not the same old Jesus, that he was somehow new? As a Christian, I confess in the Apostles' Creed that I believe in "the resurrection of the body," and when I pick away at the four Gospels' postresurrection accounts, I can't help but wonder about this resurrected body of Jesus and what it means. It's worth thinking about, especially because many Christians don't in their heart of hearts believe in the resurrection of the body. The belief of our culture is that our spirits take flight from our body after death and go to be with God. We talk in times of mourning about the body of a loved one being "just the shell."

The trouble is, that's not really what we confess. We say that our bodies matter. They're not just shells. The miracle of Christ's resurrection is that what was once as dead as the fish sticks in the supermarket freezer lives again. When we say that our bodies are nothing more than cocoons for our spirits, we're denying the sovereignty that God has over all life. God is the source of existence, and it's only by God's grace that we live.

This is not to suggest that people who believe that our spirits take flight at death aren't Christian. I myself struggle with the idea of the resurrection of the body. At the same time, however, there is a tension here in Christian thinking, and to dismiss the body as irrelevant misses something central to the faith. The body matters. Exactly how it matters I'm not sure.

There are moments when I'd like to say that the body isn't important. When I look in the mirror and see the thighs I've inherited, I'd prefer to reject the body. And on a more serious note, when I think of my mom's last days, I'd rather ignore my memories of her body. She was down to a hundred pounds; her internal organs were shot; her joints were clenched with arthritic pain. The last time I touched her hands, they were purple and puffed with fluid. They felt like cold water balloons when I held them. Mom would be better off ditching the body concept all together.

But I'm not God. I don't know what things on the other side are going to look like; however, here at the end of John, we do get a suggestion, an image, an idea. And a promise, too. In this same Gospel of John, in what is called the Farewell Discourse, Jesus told the disciples, "In my Father's house there are many dwelling places. If it were not so, would I have told you that I go to prepare a place for you? And if I go and prepare a place for you, I will come again and will take you to myself, so that where I am, you may be also" (14:2–3). As I type these words, I remember being a boy and somehow understanding for the first time that I would die someday. I couldn't sleep one night, so my mother came and sat on my bed and asked what was wrong. I told her that I was afraid to die, and though she was never a big churchgoer, she recited this line from John to me: "In my Father's house are many mansions."

I still wonder what that house will look like. What will Mom look like? What will I look like? Maybe I think too much. Maybe I'm too bound by the vision of this life. Still, I keep thinking about that unexpected teaching: the people who loved Jesus didn't recognize him at first after his resurrection. He was present with them, but he was new.

This case of Jesus' mistaken identity offers us a sacred vision. In the resurrection, we will be made new in ways we can't yet imagine. In death, we will be the same, yet changed radically. God will make something new of us, something beautiful and surprising of the old piles of joys and sufferings, successes and failures, health and injury that make up each of us. God will make something new of something old. And those who love us won't know us at first, and we won't know them. But then, every last one of us will hear Jesus speak our names, and we will know each other again. And the bodies we move, whatever they're made up of and whatever they look like, will be refreshed and cleansed, and we will hold and be held. And we'll sit together at a new table, and enjoy a meal from a new, unexpected catch of fish. And from our new bellies, we'll laugh a new laugh, and those around us will wipe away our tears of joy. And for the first time, we won't feel that empty space inside of us that longs to know God or that aching in our arms to hold and be held by God and all those we have ever loved.

Invitation to Reflection ⚬

⚘ Many of us cling to the belief that when we die, our bodies die, but our spirits live—almost independent of the will of God. What do you think about death and God's sovereignty over life?

- Why do you suppose Jesus' appearance was changed in John's postresurrection account? In addition to those noted in the meditation, what reasons come to mind for you?
- What's your dream of that day when God will breathe new life into all things?

BIBLIOGRAPHY

Brown, Robert McAfee. *Unexpected News: Reading the Bible with Third World Eyes.* Philadelphia: Westminster Press, 1984.

Culpepper, R. Alan. "The Gospel of Luke." *The New Interpreter's Bible,* Vol. IX. Nashville, Tenn.: Abingdon Press, 1995.

Grumbach, Doris. *The Presence of Absence.* Boston: Beacon Press, 1998.

Hanh, Thich Nhat. *Peace Is Every Step.* New York: Bantam Books, 1991.

Keating, Thomas, O.C.S.O. *Invitation to Love.* Rockport, Mass.: Element, 1992.

Luther's Small Catechism. (Timothy J. Wengert, trans.). Minneapolis: Augsburg Fortress, 1994.

Lutheran Book of Worship. Minneapolis: Augsburg and Philadelphia: Board of Publication, Lutheran Church in America, 1978.

Merton, Thomas. *The New Seeds of Contemplation.* New York: Norton, 1974.

Merton, Thomas. *Thoughts in Solitude.* New York: Farrar, Straus, & Giroux, 1990.

Metzger, Bruce M. *The Text of the New Testament: Its Transmission, Corruption, and Restoration.* New York: Oxford University Press, 1992.

The New Oxford Annotated Bible. New York: Oxford University Press, 1994.

Novum Testamentum Graece. (27th ed.) Stuttgart: Deutsche Bibelgesellschaft, 1993.

O'Day, Gail R. "The Gospel of John." *The New Interpreter's Bible,* Vol. 9. Nashville, Tenn.: Abingdon Press, 1995.

The Oxford Companion to the Bible. (Bruce M. Metzger and Michael D. Coogan, eds.). New York: Oxford University Press, 1993.

Powell, Mark Allan. *Fortress Introduction to the Gospels.* Minneapolis: Fortress Press, 1998.

Sobrino, Jon. *The Principle of Mercy: Taking the Crucified People from the Cross.* Maryknoll, N.Y.: Orbis, 1994.

THE AUTHOR

John Coleman is a pastor in the Evangelical Lutheran Church in America. He is the author of a collection of meditations on spirituality, *Questions from Your Cosmic Dance* (Hazelden, 1997), as well as many poems and short stories published in *The Southern Review, The Literary Review, College English,* and many other journals. Before becoming a pastor, he earned an M.A. in the Writing Seminars of Johns Hopkins University and was a college writing and literature professor for ten years. At present he serves with the people of Our Savior's Lutheran Church in Erie, Pennsylvania, where he lives with his wife, Kathy, and their two children, Elena and Micah.

INDEX

People of God, Israel as, 134
Peter (apostle): forgiveness and,
102; learning to receive and,
28–31; miraculous catch of
fish and, 5–7; rebuke by
Jesus, 33–34; transfiguration
and, 185–188
Pharisees: Jesus as Messiah and,
55–59; laws of purity and,
129; Sabbath and, 154–155;
specifics of law and, 61–62
Philippians 4:7, 151
Pity, 51–52
Poverty, 49, 58
Powell, M. A., 104
Prayer: answering of, 94–96,
173–175; Jesus and, 166–169;
Lord's Prayer, 132–137; mak-
ing time for, 11–15
Presence of Absence, The
(Grumbach), 15, 152

R
Receiving and giving, 28–31, 64
Reigning of God, 62–65
Resurrection, of Jesus, 227
Resurrection, of the body,
225–227
Romans 3:23, 120
Romans 7:15, 136
Romero, O., 57–58
Root, M., 95

S
Sabbath: as gift from God,
22–25; interpretation of, 79;
Pharisees and, 154–155
Samaritan woman, 42, 143, 183,
194–200

Sarah, 35
Satan, and temptations of Jesus,
176–178
Scripture: interpretation of, 49,
77–78, 79; misuse of,
103–104; money lending in,
106–107; origins of, 75–78;
selective reading of, 17; slav-
ery in, 106–107; as teacher,
35–36. *See also individual
books of Scripture*; Miracles;
Parables
Security, detachment from,
177–181
Self, transformation of, 7, 8
Sermon on the Mount, 86
Service, as response to God's
blessings, 111–114
Shame, healing of, 138–145
Silence, need for, 189
Simon Peter (apostle). *See* Peter
(apostle)
Simon's mother-in-law, 110–114
Sin, concepts of, 43–44, 135–136
Slavery, 44, 106–107
Small Catechism (Luther), 68,
135, 212–213
Sobrino, J., 49, 119, 154
Soul and body, healing of, 94–95
Soul, needs of, 178–181
Suffering: endurance of, 161–163;
Jesus and, 17–20, 166–169;
liberation theology and, 49

T
Temptations of Jesus, in wilder-
ness, 176–181
Theology of the cross, 168–169
Thoreau, H. D., 179–180